50 fantastic recipes with

just four
ingredients

50 fantastic recipes with just four ingredients

step-by-step dishes for every occasion

JOANNA FARROW

HERMES HOUSE

This edition is published by Hermes House

Hermes House is an imprint of Anness Publishing Ltd
Hermes House, 88–89 Blackfriars Road, London SE1 8HA
tel. 020 7401 2077; fax 020 7633 9499; info@anness.com

A CIP catalogue record for this book is available from the British Library.

Publisher: Joanna Lorenz
Editor: Elizabeth Woodland
Senior Editor: Susannah Blake
Production Controller: Darren Price
Photography: Tim Auty, Martin Brigdale, Nicky Dowey, Gus Filgate, Michelle Garrett, Amanda Heywood, William Lingwood, Craig Robertson, Simon Smith
Recipes: Alex Barker, Jacqueline Clark, Joanna Farrow, Brian Glover, Jane Milton, Jennie Shapter, Marlena Spieler, Kate Whiteman

Previously published as *Under 10 With 4 or Less*

10 9 8 7 6 5 4 3 2 1

NOTES

Bracketed terms are intended for American readers.

For all recipes, quantities are given in both metric and imperial measures and, where appropriate, measures are also given in standard cups and spoons. Follow one set, but not a mixture, because they are not interchangeable.

Standard spoon and cup measures are level.

1 tsp = 5ml, 1 tbsp = 15ml, 1 cup = 250ml/8fl oz

Australian standard tablespoons are 20ml. Australian readers should use 3 tsp in place of 1 tbsp for measuring small quantities of gelatine, flour, salt, etc.

Medium (US large) eggs are used unless otherwise stated.

The very young, elderly and those in ill-health or with a compromised immune system are advised against consuming raw eggs or dishes containing raw eggs.

Contents

Fast Food, Few Ingredients

It sounds like the sort of challenge a TV producer would love – make a delicious meal in under ten minutes using no more than four ingredients. Can it be done? Well, here's the proof – more than seventy superb dishes, from snacks to sweet treats. Starting with dips, sauces and salads, the recipes include great vegetarian choices, quick meat and fish meals, tasty pasta dishes, and side dishes that could easily relinquish their supporting roles to become main attractions. Add a nourishing smoothie or fresh juice from the selection at the back of the book. Producing good food fast has never been easier.

Less to carry home

Using a limited number of top-quality ingredients makes shopping effortless. There's no lengthy list to write, no heavy trolley to push and less to carry home. This is a particular boon to those who travel by bus or bicycle, or who have to walk back from the shops. Having only a small number of ingredients simplifies storage, too. If you're a student, sharing a kitchen, this can be a real bonus.

Savour the flavour

When you're cooking with four ingredients, you really get to savour the individual flavours, so it is important to buy the best quality ingredients you can find. Be selective when buying, as the better the raw materials, the finer will be the flavour of the finished dish. Top-quality produce will also need fewer additional herbs, spices or condiments to make it taste fabulous.

The best for less

Buying the best does not necessarily mean paying more. For example, meat from a good traditional-style butcher is often cheaper than the supermarket equivalent, and because local butchers are able to source their stock from small suppliers who really know their meat, it may well have a fuller flavour. For recipes that cook in 10 minutes or less, you need tender cuts like pork, lamb or beef fillet (tenderloin), or chicken breast portions. Lamb's liver is a very good buy. It is a good idea to keep packs of frozen lamb's liver in the freezer. Transfer to the refrigerator early in the day to thaw slowly, and the trimmed slices will be ready to cook for dinner. Fried liver with bacon and onions makes a delicious quick meal, especially if you serve it with polenta and fine green beans. Chicken livers are tasty and inexpensive, too. Try them sautéed with a dash of Tabasco, and serve them on toast or on top of tossed salad leaves.

Using good quality fruit and vegetables adds to the flavour of dishes.

From left: Red mullet, trout and salmon.

Finding good fish

Good fish can be slightly harder to locate. Be choosy when buying from supermarket fish counters: avoid tired-looking specimens and remember that it is better to go for good-quality frozen fish and shellfish rather than poor-quality fresh. All fish cooks quickly, but for a real flash in the pan, choose shellfish such as scallops or prawns (shrimp). If you live near the sea, and can buy straight from the fishing boats, tailor your cooking to the catch of the day, rather than attempting to buy varieties that are scarce and therefore expensive. Coley is an excellent fish – the rather unattractive grey flesh becomes beautifully white when cooked, and it tastes very good. Huss, pollock and whiting are very good value, and for speedy cooking dabs and other small members of the flounder family are ideal. Don't forget mackerel and herring, which have oils that can help to reduce the risk of coronary heart disease.

The fresher the better

Cauliflower, Savoy cabbage, Brussels sprouts, spinach leaves, broccoli and kale.

Vegetables and fruit are a gift to the quick cook using just a few ingredients. Salads need no cooking at all, and stir-fries and steamed dishes take very little time. When shopping for vegetables, bear in mind that the fresher the produce, the higher will be the vitamin content. Farmers' markets are a good source of fresh produce, as are pick-your-own farms and those roadside stalls where gardeners sell their surplus fruit and vegetables. If you can't obtain very fresh vegetables, it is sometimes better to opt for frozen vegetables, which are picked and processed at the peak of perfection.

Stocks and sauces

Ready-made stocks and sauces are infinitely useful for creating quick and easy meals, and are a great way to cut down on preparation and cooking time. A basic tomato sauce tastes great with poached fish or grilled (broiled) steak, or can be tossed with pasta or potato gnocchi. For a quick vegetarian treat, mix lightly cooked broccoli and cauliflower florets with home-made tomato sauce, top with grated cheese and brown under the grill (broiler).

A basic vegetable stock is easy to make and can be stored in the refrigerator for up to four days. Alternatively, make large quantities and store in the freezer.

Pesto provides another simple solution to the question of what to serve for supper when speed is of the essence. Try it with tagliatelle or in risotto. On a sweet note, a good quality ready-made custard makes an excellent base for an ice cream, as well as a tasty accompaniment to fresh fruit.

Good-quality bought sauces are readily available fresh or in jars – check out the list of ingredients on the pack for some indication of the quality.

A good bought liquid concentrate or fresh stock is worth keeping in the refrigerator or freezer. Remember that many bought chilled fresh products are suitable for home freezing, which is a good way of extending their shelf life. Alternatively, you can make your own supply of basic stocks and sauces in large quantities and freeze them in convenient, ready-to-use batches.

Storecupboard Essentials

The recipes in this book take a minimalist approach, with a small number of ingredients cooked in the shortest possible time. They're so quick and easy that you'll want to return to them again and again, ringing the changes by introducing new flavourings from your selectively stocked storecupboard or pantry.

A well-stocked storecupboard should include all the basic staples, such as sugar, eggs and fruit.

Oil and Vinegar

Every kitchen needs at least two types of oil – a good quality olive oil and a light vegetable oil for cooking. Extra virgin olive oil is good in dressings and robust Mediterranean dishes, when its flavour will make a positive contribution, but if you are cooking something more subtle, choose a lighter olive oil or sunflower oil. A nut oil such as walnut or hazelnut works well in a salad dressing, and chilli oil is great for spicy foods. Buy oils in small quantities and store them in a cool, dark place. Although it is tempting to stand bottles of oil next to the stove, where they are handy, this is the worst place for them, since excessive heat can cause the oil to spoil.

White wine vinegar is excellent for salad dressings. For a more intense flavour, buy balsamic vinegar, but don't overdo its use. A little balsamic dripped into olive oil makes a great dip for bread, and it can also be used in much the same way as wine, to enrich the flavour of a meat dish. This type of vinegar also goes well with strawberries.

From left: Walnut, sesame and hazelnut oils.

Preserved or dried vegetables

Like balsamic vinegar, sun-dried tomatoes should be used with care, but they do have a marvellous taste. For convenience, buy the ones that come packed in oil. They may be more expensive, but the oil is a useful ingredient in its own right. Use it for frying aromatics like onions or garlic when you are making a pasta sauce, and toss a little with the cooked pasta just before serving.

Sun-dried tomatoes bottled in oil with dry pieces.

Also useful are jars of roasted (bell) peppers, capers, caper berries and both sweet and hot chillies. A tube of tomato purée (paste) is an indispensable ingredient. A quick squeeze will intensify the flavour of a soup or sauce. Dried mushrooms bring a full flavour to mushroom dishes and can be good for perking up simple soups, sauces or risottos.

Canned goods

Where space is at a premium, storing cans can be a problem, but it is always worth having on hand some canned tomatoes. For speed, choose chopped tomatoes in tomato sauce, and opt for organic tomatoes if you can find them. For economy, choose canned whole plum tomatoes and use a potato masher to pulp them into your sauce. Also useful are canned lentils and beans, corn kernels, artichoke hearts, tuna and anchovies. For speedy desserts, canned fruits are very useful. Canned passion-fruit pulp, for instance, is delicious in fresh fruit salads, and canned apricots can be whizzed up in a blender, then spooned over ice cream or poached pears.

Canned beans are useful storecupboard stand-bys. The beans tend to be softer than home-cooked, dried beans and can be used to make quick salads.

Coriander (cilantro) has its own unique flavour. For best results use the stem and leaves as soon as possible after purchase.

Herbs and spices

The quickest way to alter the signature of a dish is to add a sympathetic herb or spice. The ideal is to have herbs growing in your garden – or even in a pot on a windowsill – as they do lose flavour quite quickly after being picked. Dried herbs and spices deteriorate rapidly once they are exposed to the air, so it is best to buy small quantities. If you do buy a large packet, decant a small amount into a spice jar and store the remainder in the freezer. If possible, buy spices like cumin and coriander whole and grind them as needed using a mortar and pestle or spice grinder. Freshly grated whole nutmeg is better than ready ground, and adds interest to potato dishes, custards and white sauces.

Spices and herbs can be ground together to form flavourful pastes.

Sauces

It is useful to have a small selection of sauces such as Worcestershire, Tabasco and soy sauce, plus pesto, for perking up simple dishes. For a quick snack using just three ingredients, place thick slices of mature (sharp) Cheddar cheese or Monterey Jack on toast, drizzle with Worcestershire sauce and grill (broil) until bubbly. Tabasco mixed with melted butter and lime juice makes a great basting sauce for pork fillet (tenderloin) and soy sauce tastes superb in stir-fries, salad dressings and gravies.

From left: Nam pla, Worcestershire sauce and anchovy essence.

Dry goods

Other essential storecupboard ingredients include salt and pepper (preferably as peppercorns in a mill, so that it can be ground as needed). Sugar, flour and cornflour (cornstarch) are staples, and you will also need long grain and risotto rice and pasta. For cooking in under 10 minutes, fresh pasta is preferable, but it is also possible to buy dried pasta that cooks quickly. Don't forget noodles, many of which need no cooking at all, but are simply softened in hot water before being used.

Hemp spaghetti, gluten-free corn spaghetti and spiralina tagliatelle.

Using the recipes

Each recipe uses no more than four ingredients, excluding salt, pepper and water. A ready-made stock or sauce is sometimes included, but you can always substitute a home-made one if you prefer. Serving suggestions and ideas for garnishes or decorations are included where appropriate, but these are not essential for the success of the dish. There are also suggestions for variations or additional flavourings and handy cook's tips that will help you achieve successful results every time.

QUICK COOK'S TIPS

When you're preparing a meal with minimum ingredients in the shortest possible time, offering an appetizer or ending with a dessert may seem like attempting the impossible. It can be done – just cheat a little:

- *Instead of an appetizer, serve chunks of bread with extra virgin olive oil. Better still, flavour the oil with zahtar – a spice blend of toasted sesame seeds, sumac berries and thyme – or invite guests to dip the bread into the oil and then into dukkah – a flavoursome Egyptian mixture including sesame seeds, roasted hazelnuts, coriander and cumin.*
- *Arrange squares of feta cheese, cherry tomatoes, kalamata olives and cucumber sticks on a platter. Offer cocktail sticks (toothpicks) as eating utensils.*
- *Make Eton Mess: beat cream until stiff, then fold in halved strawberries. Roughly break up good-quality bought meringues and add them to the mixture. Stir and serve immediately.*

Equipment for simple, speedy cooking

As anyone who has ever been camping will know, it is surprising how few utensils and items of equipment you need to produce a good meal. Two or three sharp knives, a couple of decent pans, and a mixing bowl and a spoon are the bare essentials, but for speedy preparation and cooking, a few extras will prove invaluable.

Knives

Good-quality knives are a must. It is much better to have two really good knives than a matched set of mediocre ones. With a small, sharp vegetable knife and a cook's knife, you can do most basic preparation. Buy more knives when you can afford them. Store knives in a knife rack or wallet for safety and to protect the blades, and sharpen frequently. You can chop or dice food faster and more efficiently with a sharp knife than a blunt blade.

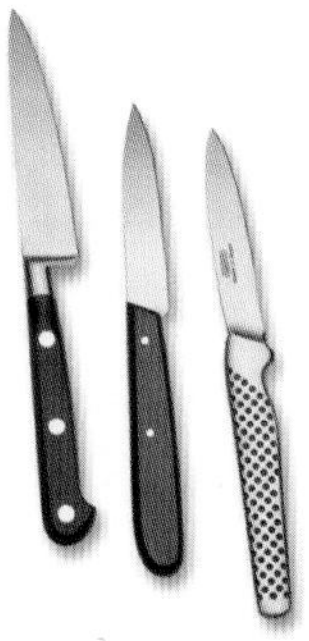

Paring knives.

Chopping Board

When chopping meat or fish, use a plastic board. A large, heavy wooden board is a good choice for preparing vegetables and fruit, as it will not slip while in use. Avoid glass boards, because they blunt knives quickly.

Pans

For fast cooking with just a few ingredients, a wok is ideal, especially if it will double as a steamer. You will also need two or three pans of various sizes. Choose heavy pans, as food cooked in them is less likely to burn, even at high temperatures. You will need a large, heavy frying pan. Quick cooks also benefit from having a crêpe pan, because pancakes are an ideal choice when preparing food quickly with just a few ingredients.

Single-handled woks are easy to hold when stir-frying, whereas double-handled ones may be more stable for deep-frying.

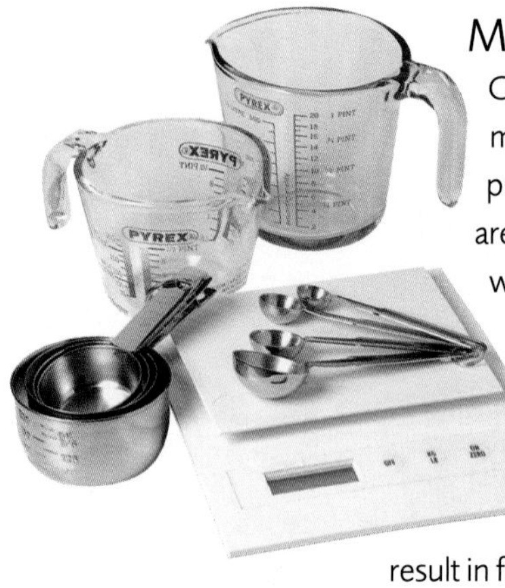

Using scales and measuring jugs, cups and spoons is essential for good results.

Measuring aids

Good kitchen scales, measuring cups and proper spoon measures are essential, especially when preparing cakes or similar recipes where even small deviations from the suggested quantities may result in failure. If you are a kitchen novice, using the exact amounts recommended in recipes will ensure good results and help you become a successful and confident cook.

Several different types of scales are available, from spring and balance models to digital scales, which are extremely accurate. In several countries, cooks use cups for dry and wet ingredients. This method works well for most recipes, but because the sets of cups are not standardized, results can vary. When measuring liquids, use heatproof jugs or pitchers marked with metric and imperial measures. For small quantities, use metal measuring spoons. These come in sets, ranging from 1.5ml/¼ tsp to 15ml/1 tbsp. Do not use spoons that are intended for eating or serving food, as the bowls of these spoons do vary widely in volume.

Electrical equipment

When it comes to preparing and cooking food fast, there's nothing more useful than a food processor This appliance takes all the effort out of chopping, blending, grating and making dips, purées, smoothies and soothing drinks. If your processor has a small bowl that can be seated inside the large one for small quantities, you'll save time on washing up, too. Also very useful is a blender wand or hand-held blender that processes ingredients in a pan or bowl. Like a goblet blender, this appliance reduces soups to a finer texture than can be obtained by using a food processor. An electric whisk is practical for whipping cream, whisking egg whites, creaming cakes and producing smooth mashed or creamed potato.

Blenders are perfect for preparing fast food.

Tips and Techniques

For fast-track food, the trick is to keep it simple. If you can avoid cooking altogether, so much the better, so choose dips, salads, cold desserts or nourishing drinks where possible. Prime candidates for quick cooking are soups and pasta dishes, stir-fries, grills and steamed foods.

Frying

When you are cooking with a limited number of ingredients, this is an excellent method to use, as it encourages browning and caramelization on the surface of the food, enhancing the natural flavours. The cooked food will often require nothing more than a squeeze of lemon juice or sprinkling of ground pepper to complete the dish.

Pan-frying

The initial frying of ingredients can help to determine the final character of a dish. Heat the oil before adding the ingredients and do not add too much at once. Overfilling the pan will steam or braise, rather than fry, the food. If necessary, pan-fry ingredients in batches.

Stir-frying

This uses less oil than traditional frying methods and is very rapid, ideal for quick dishes with few ingredients. The juices yielded are usually sufficient to form a sauce.

Deep-frying

As the name suggests, this involves using sufficient oil to submerge the ingredients to be cooked. It is important that the oil has reached the correct temperature before the food is added. Check by adding a cube of bread. It should turn golden in 60 seconds. Delicate ingredients are often coated in egg and breadcrumbs or batter before being deep-fried.

Dry-frying

This is achieved by using a non-stick pan. No oil is required, which is helpful when you are trying to reduce the number of cooking ingredients.

Grilling

Cooking under a grill (broiler) or on a griddle imparts a rich, smoky flavour to food. Tender cuts of meat, poultry, fish, shellfish and vegetables need little more than light seasoning and brushing with oil. Preheat the grill or pan before cooking the food and baste non-fatty foods with oil, a marinade or a basting mixture during grilling (broiling) to prevent them from drying out. If cooking on a griddle, oil the food, not the pan, or a great deal of smoke will be generated.

Steaming

Perhaps the purest form of cooking, this doesn't impart flavour in the way that frying or grilling does, but lets the natural taste of the food come through. Choose good-quality ingredients that are not too dense and you may be surprised at how quickly they cook. Steamed food can be served *au naturel* or with an interesting sauce or accompaniment.

QUICK COOK'S TIPS

- *Drain a jar of pickled sweet cherry chillies. Fill the chillies with full-fat soft cheese.*
- *For a quick dessert, buy ready-sliced fresh pineapple from the supermarket, sprinkle with brown sugar and grill (broil) until golden. Serve with vanilla ice cream.*
- *Cut just-ripe figs into quarters. Pile in glasses and sprinkle with your favourite orange liqueur.*
- *Make a simple dip by mixing cream cheese with finely chopped fresh parsley. Serve with strips of pitta bread as dippers.*

Snacks and Appetizers

THE PERFECT SNACK OR APPETIZER SHOULD LOOK FANTASTIC, TASTE DELICIOUS AND REQUIRE THE MINIMUM OF EFFORT TO PREPARE. THE RECIPES IN THIS CHAPTER DO JUST THAT, BRINGING TOGETHER DELICIOUS COMBINATIONS OF FLAVOURS, TEXTURES, AROMAS AND COLOURS TO WHET THE APPETITE BEFORE THE MAIN COURSE.

Creamy Garlic Dip

This classic, creamy garlic mayonnaise from France is simple to make and absolutely delicious. Serve it with salads or as a dip with crudités, with potato wedges, or as a quick sauce for pan-fried salmon. Try to use extra virgin olive oil for this mayonnaise if you can – it has a rich and delicious flavour that really makes this sauce special.

SERVES FOUR TO SIX

1 Put the garlic cloves in a mortar, add a pinch of salt and pound to a smooth paste with a pestle.

2 Transfer the garlic paste to a bowl. Add the egg yolks and whisk for about 30 seconds, until creamy. Whisk in the olive oil, drop by drop, until the mixture begins to thicken, then add the oil in a slow drizzle until the mixture is thick and creamy.

3 Beat in the lemon juice and seasoning to taste. Serve immediately or cover with clear film (plastic wrap) and chill in the refrigerator until ready to use. Allow the dip to return to room temperature before serving.

4 large garlic cloves, peeled

2 egg yolks

250ml/8fl oz/1 cup extra virgin olive oil

15–30ml/1–2 tbsp lemon juice

Watercress Sauce

This pretty green sauce is refreshingly tart and peppery. It is delicious served as an accompaniment to poached fish, or as a dip for simply grilled prawns (shrimp). Do not prepare the sauce more than a few hours ahead of serving, as the watercress will discolour the sauce. This peppery green sauce can also be made with rocket (arugula) leaves instead of the watercress.

SERVES SIX TO EIGHT

200g/7oz watercress leaves

300g/11oz/1¼ cups mayonnaise

15–30ml/1–2 tbsp freshly squeezed lemon juice

200g/7oz/scant 1 cup unsalted (sweet) butter

1 Remove the tough stems from the watercress leaves and finely chop the leaves by hand or in a food processor. Add the mayonnaise and the freshly squeezed lemon juice and process to mix.

2 Melt the unsalted butter, then add to the watercress mixture, a little at a time, processing or whisking in a bowl until the butter has been fully incorporated and the sauce is thick and smooth. Season to taste with salt and pepper, then cover and chill in the refrigerator before serving.

EXTRAS

Garlic makes a delicious addition to this sauce. Peel and finely chop 1–2 garlic cloves and combine with the chopped watercress leaves, mayonnaise and lemon juice, before adding the melted butter in step 2.

Hummus

This classic Middle Eastern chickpea dip is flavoured with garlic and tahini (sesame seed paste). A little ground cumin can also be added, and olive oil can be stirred in to enrich the hummus, if you like. It is delicious served with wedges of toasted pitta bread or crudités.

SERVES FOUR TO SIX

1 Using a potato masher or fork, coarsely mash the chickpeas in a mixing bowl. If you like a smoother purée, process the chickpeas in a food processor or blender until a smooth paste is formed.

2 Mix the tahini into the bowl of chickpeas, then stir in the chopped garlic cloves and lemon juice. Season to taste with freshly ground black pepper and salt, and if needed, add a little water. Serve the hummus at room temperature.

400g/14oz can chickpeas, drained

60ml/4 tbsp tahini

2–3 garlic cloves, chopped

juice of ½–1 lemon

EXTRAS

Process 2 roasted red (bell) peppers with the chickpeas, then continue as above. Serve sprinkled with lightly toasted pine nuts and paprika mixed with olive oil.

Mushroom Caviar

The name caviar refers to the dark colour and texture of this dish of chopped mushrooms. Serve the mushroom mixture in individual serving dishes with toasted rye bread rubbed with cut garlic cloves, to accompany. Chopped hard-boiled egg, spring onion and parsley, the traditional garnishes for caviar, can be added as a garnish.

SERVES FOUR

1 Heat the oil in a large pan, add the mushrooms, shallots and garlic, and cook, stirring occasionally, until browned. Season with salt, then continue cooking until the mushrooms give up their liquor.

2 Continue cooking, stirring frequently, until the liquor has evaporated and the mushrooms are brown and dry.

3 Put the mixture in a food processor or blender and process briefly until a chunky paste is formed. Spoon the mushroom caviar into dishes and serve.

45ml/3 tbsp olive or vegetable oil

450g/1lb mushrooms, coarsely chopped

5–10 shallots, chopped

4 garlic cloves, chopped

EXTRAS

For a rich wild mushroom caviar, soak 10–15g/¼–½oz dried porcini in about 120ml/4fl oz/ ½ cup water for about 30 minutes. Add the porcini and their soaking liquid to the browned mushrooms in step 2. Continue as in the recipe. Serve with wedges of lemon, for their tangy juice.

Eggs Mimosa

Mimosa describes the fine yellow and white grated egg in this dish, which looks very similar to the flower of the same name. The eggs taste delicious when garnished with black pepper and basil leaves. Grated egg yolk can also be used as a garnish for a variety of other savoury dishes, such as sauces, soups and rice dishes.

MAKES TWENTY

1 Reserve two of the hard-boiled eggs and halve the remainder. Carefully remove the yolks with a teaspoon and blend them with the avocados, garlic and oil, adding freshly ground black pepper and salt to taste. Spoon or pipe the mixture into the halved egg whites using a piping (pastry) bag with a 1cm/½in or pipe star nozzle.

2 Sieve the remaining egg whites and sprinkle over the filled eggs. Sieve the yolks and arrange on top. Arrange the filled egg halves on a serving platter.

12 eggs, hard-boiled and peeled

2 ripe avocados, halved and stoned (pitted)

1 garlic clove, crushed

15ml/1 tbsp olive oil

COOK'S TIP

You can prepare the mimosa garnish in advance and keep it in the refrigerator. Do not combine the egg white and yolk at this stage, but store in separate, airtight containers.

Japanese-style Spinach with Toasted Sesame Seeds

This Japanese speciality, known as *O-hitashi*, has been served as a side dish on dining tables in Japan for centuries. Seasonal green vegetables are simply blanched and cooled and formed into little towers. With a little help from soy sauce and sesame seeds, they reveal their true flavour. Serve the spinach towers with simply cooked chicken or fish, such as salmon or tuna.

SERVES FOUR

450g/1lb fresh young spinach

30ml/2 tbsp shoyu

30ml/2 tbsp water

15ml/1 tbsp sesame seeds

1 Blanch the spinach leaves in lightly salted boiling water for 15 seconds. For Japanese-type spinach, hold the leafy part and slip the stems into the pan. After 15 seconds, drop in the leaves and cook for 20 seconds.

2 Drain immediately and place the spinach under running water. Squeeze out all the excess water by hand. Now what looked like a large amount of spinach has become a ball, roughly the size of an orange. Mix the shoyu and water, then pour on to the spinach. Mix well and leave to cool.

3 Meanwhile, put the sesame seeds in a dry frying pan and stir or toss until they start to pop. Remove from the heat and leave to cool.

4 Drain the spinach and squeeze out the excess sauce with your hands. Form the spinach into a log shape of about 4cm/1½in in diameter on a chopping board. Squeeze again to make it firm. With a sharp knife, cut it across into four cylinders.

5 Place the spinach cylinders on a large plate or individual dishes. Sprinkle with the toasted sesame seeds and a little salt and serve.

COOK'S TIP

Japanese spinach, the long-leaf type with the stalks and pink root intact, is best, but you can use ordinary young spinach leaves, or any soft and deep-green salad leaves – such as watercress, rocket (arugula) or lamb's lettuce.

Figs with Prosciutto and Roquefort

Fresh figs are a delicious treat, whether you choose dark purple, yellowy green or green-skinned varieties. When they are ripe, you can split them open with your fingers to reveal the soft, sweet flesh full of edible seeds. In this easy, stylish dish figs and honey balance the richness of the ham and cheese. Serve with warm bread for a simple appetizer before any rich main course.

SERVES FOUR

8 fresh figs

75g/3oz prosciutto

45ml/3 tbsp clear honey

75g/3oz Roquefort cheese

1 Preheat the grill (broiler). Quarter the figs and place on a foil-lined grill rack. Tear each slice of prosciutto into two or three pieces and crumple them up on the foil beside the figs. Brush the figs with 15ml/1 tbsp of the clear honey and cook under the grill until lightly browned.

2 Crumble the Roquefort cheese and divide among four plates, setting it to one side. Add the honey-grilled figs and ham and pour over any cooking juices caught on the foil. Drizzle the remaining honey over the figs, ham and cheese, and serve seasoned with plenty of freshly ground black pepper.

Walnut and Goat's Cheese Bruschetta

The combination of toasted walnuts and melting goat's cheese is lovely in this simple appetizer, served with a pile of salad leaves. Toasting the walnuts helps to enhance their flavour. Walnut bread is readily available in most large supermarkets and makes an interesting alternative to ordinary crusty bread, although this can be used if walnut bread is unavailable.

SERVES FOUR

1 Preheat the grill (broiler). Lightly toast the walnut pieces, then remove and set aside. Put the walnut bread on a foil-lined grill rack and toast on one side. Turn the slices over and drizzle each with 15ml/1 tbsp of the French dressing.

2 Cut the goat's cheese into twelve slices and place three on each piece of bread. Grill (broil) for about 3 minutes, until the cheese is melting and beginning to brown.

3 Transfer the bruschetta to serving plates, sprinkle with the toasted walnuts and drizzle with the remaining French dressing. Serve the bruschetta immediately with salad leaves.

50g/2oz/½ cup walnut pieces

4 thick slices walnut bread

120ml/4fl oz/½ cup French dressing

200g/7oz chèvre or other semi-soft goat's cheese

COOK'S TIP

Use walnut bread slices from a slender loaf, so that the portions are not too wide. If you can buy only a large loaf, cut the slices in half to make neat, chunky pieces.

Sour Cucumber with Fresh Dill

This is half pickle, half salad, and totally delicious served with pumpernickel or other coarse, dark, full-flavoured bread, as a light meal or an appetizer. Choose smooth-skinned, smallish cucumbers for this recipe as larger ones tend to be less tender, with tough skins and bitter indigestible seeds. If you can only buy a large cucumber, peel it before slicing.

SERVES FOUR

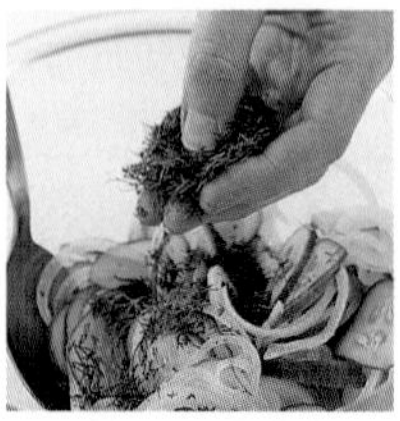

2 small cucumbers, thinly sliced

3 onions, thinly sliced

75–90ml/5–6 tbsp cider vinegar

30–45ml/2–3 tbsp chopped fresh dill

1 In a large mixing bowl, combine together the thinly sliced cucumbers and the thinly sliced onion. Season the vegetables with salt and toss together until they are thoroughly combined. Leave the mixture to stand in a cool place for 5–10 minutes.

2 Add the cider vinegar, 30–45ml/2–3 tbsp water and the chopped fresh dill to the cucumber and onion mixture. Toss all the ingredients together until well combined, then chill in the refrigerator for a few hours, or until ready to serve.

EXTRAS

For a sweet and sour mixture, add 45ml/3 tbsp caster (superfine) sugar with the cider vinegar in step 2.

Pink Grapefruit and Avocado Salad

Smooth, creamy avocado and zesty citrus fruit are perfect partners in an attractive, refreshing salad. Pink grapefruit are tangy but not too sharp, or try large oranges for a sweeter flavour. Avocados turn brown quickly when exposed to the air: the acidic grapefruit juice will prevent this from occurring, so combine the ingredients as soon as the avocados have been sliced.

SERVES FOUR

2 pink grapefruit

2 ripe avocados

30ml/2 tbsp chilli oil

90g/3½oz rocket (arugula)

1 Slice the top and bottom off a grapefruit, then cut off all the peel and pith from around the side. Working over a small bowl to catch the juices, cut out the segments from between the membranes and place them in a separate bowl. Squeeze any juices remaining in the membranes into the bowl, then discard them. Repeat with the remaining grapefruit.

2 Halve, stone (pit) and peel the avocados. Slice the flesh and add it to the grapefruit segments. Whisk a little salt and then the chilli oil into the grapefruit juice.

3 Pile the rocket leaves on to four serving plates and top with the grapefruit segments and avocado. Pour over the dressing and serve. Alternatively, toss the rocket with the grapefruit, avocado and dressing, then divide the salad among plates or bowls.

Tomato, Bean and Fried Basil Salad

Infusing basil in hot oil brings out its wonderful, aromatic flavour, which works so well in almost any tomato dish. Various canned beans or chickpeas can be used instead of mixed beans in this simple dish, as they all taste good and make a wholesome salad to serve as an accompaniment or a satisfying snack with some warm, grainy bread.

SERVES FOUR

1 Reserve one-third of the basil leaves for garnish, then tear the remainder into pieces. Pour the olive oil into a small pan. Add the torn basil and heat gently for 1 minute, until the basil sizzles and begins to colour.

2 Place the halved cherry tomatoes and beans in a bowl. Pour in the basil oil and add a little salt and plenty of freshly ground black pepper. Toss the ingredients together gently, cover and leave to marinate at room temperature for 7–8 minutes. Serve the salad sprinkled with the remaining basil leaves.

15g/½oz/½ cup fresh basil leaves

75ml/5 tbsp extra virgin olive oil

300g/11oz cherry tomatoes, halved

400g/14oz can mixed beans, drained and rinsed

Summer Squash and Baby New Potatoes in Warm Dill Sour Cream

Fresh vegetables and fragrant dill are delicious tossed in a simple sour cream or yogurt sauce. Choose small squash with bright skins that are free from blemishes and bruises. To make a simpler potato salad, pour the dill sour cream over warm cooked potatoes. Serve either version of the potato salad with poached salmon or chargrilled chicken.

SERVES FOUR

400g/14oz mixed squash, such as yellow and green courgettes (zucchini), and pale green patty pan

400g/14oz tiny, baby new potatoes

1 large handful mixed fresh dill and chives, finely chopped

300ml/½ pint/1¼ cups sour cream or Greek (US strained plain) yogurt

1 Cut the squash into pieces about the same size as the potatoes. Put the potatoes in a pan and add water to cover and a pinch of salt. Bring to the boil, then simmer for about 10 minutes, until almost tender. Add the squash and continue to cook until the vegetables are just tender, then drain.

2 Put the vegetables into a wide, shallow pan and gently stir in the finely chopped fresh dill and chives.

3 Remove the pan from the heat and stir in the sour cream or yogurt. Return to the heat and heat gently until warm. Season and serve.

Light Meals

THIS SELECTION OF RECIPES IS INCREDIBLY EASY TO MAKE AND USES ONLY A FEW INGREDIENTS AND FLAVOURINGS TO CREATE FABULOUS, MOUTHWATERING RESULTS. FROM SIMPLE PASTA DISHES TO WARMING WINTER BROTHS, THESE DELICIOUS DISHES ARE IDEAL FOR ANYONE WHO DESIRES A LIGHT LUNCH OR SUPPER.

Avocado Soup

This delicious soup has a fresh, delicate flavour and a wonderful colour. For added zest, add a generous squeeze of lime juice or spoon 15ml/1 tbsp salsa into the soup just before serving. Choose ripe avocados for this soup – they should feel soft when gently pressed. Keep very firm avocados at room temperature for 3–4 days until they soften. To speed ripening, place in a brown paper bag.

SERVES FOUR

2 large ripe avocados

300ml/½ pint/1¼ cups sour cream

1 litre/1¾ pints/ 4 cups well-flavoured chicken stock

small bunch of fresh coriander (cilantro)

1 Cut the avocados in half, remove the peel and lift out the stones (pits). Chop the flesh coarsely and place it in a food processor with 45–60ml/3–4 tbsp of the sour cream. Process until smooth.

2 Heat the chicken stock in a pan. When it is hot, but still below simmering point, stir in the rest of the cream with salt to taste.

3 Gradually stir the avocado mixture into the hot stock. Heat gently but do not let the mixture approach boiling point.

4 Chop the coriander. Ladle the soup into individual heated bowls and sprinkle each portion with chopped coriander and black pepper. Serve immediately.

Stilton and Watercress Soup

A good creamy Stilton and plenty of peppery watercress bring maximum flavour to this rich, smooth soup, which is superlative in small portions. Rocket (arugula) can be used as an alternative to watercress – both leaves are an excellent source of iron. When choosing any salad leaves, look for crisp, fresh leaves and reject any wilted or discoloured greens.

SERVES FOUR TO SIX

1 Pour the stock into a pan and bring almost to the boil. Remove and discard any very large stalks from the watercress. Add the watercress to the pan and simmer gently for 2–3 minutes, until tender.

2 Crumble the cheese into the pan and simmer for 1 minute more, until the cheese has started to melt. Process the soup in a blender or food processor, in batches if necessary, until very smooth. Return the soup to the pan.

3 Stir in the cream and check the seasoning. The soup will probably not need any extra salt, as the blue cheese is already quite salty. Heat the soup gently, without boiling, then ladle it into warm bowls.

600ml/1 pint/ 2½ cups chicken or vegetable stock

225g/8oz watercress

150g/5oz Stilton or other blue cheese

150ml/¼ pint/⅔ cup single (light) cream

Butter Bean, Sun-dried Tomato and Pesto Soup

This soup is so quick and easy to make: the key is to use a good-quality home-made or bought fresh stock for the best result. Using plenty of pesto and sun-dried tomato purée (paste) gives it a rich, minestrone-like flavour. As an alternative to butter beans, haricot (navy) or cannellini beans will make good substitutes.

SERVES FOUR

1 Put the stock in a pan with the butter beans and bring just to the boil. Reduce the heat and stir in the tomato purée and pesto. Cook gently for 5 minutes.

2 Transfer six ladlefuls of the soup to a blender or food processor, scooping up plenty of the beans. Process until smooth, then return the purée to the pan.

3 Heat gently, stirring frequently, for 5 minutes, then season if necessary. Ladle into four warmed soup bowls and serve with warm crusty bread or breadsticks.

900ml/1½ pints/ 3¾ cups chicken or vegetable stock

2 x 400g/14oz cans butter (lima) beans, drained and rinsed

60ml/4 tbsp sun-dried tomato purée (paste)

75ml/5 tbsp pesto

Avgolemono

The name of this popular Greek soup means egg and lemon, the two essential ingredients that produce a light, nourishing soup. The soup also contains orzo, which is Greek, rice-shaped pasta, but you can use any small shape. Serve the soup with thin slices of lightly toasted bread and add a garnish of very thin lemon slices for a pretty appearance on special occasions.

SERVES FOUR TO SIX

1.75 litres/3 pints/ 7½ cups chicken stock

115g/4oz/½ cup orzo pasta

3 eggs

juice of 1 large lemon

1 Pour the chicken stock into a large pan and bring to the boil. Add the orzo pasta or other small pasta shapes and cook for 5 minutes, or according to the packet instructions.

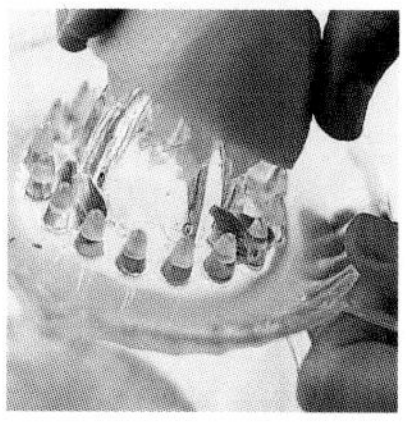

2 Beat the eggs until they are frothy, then add the lemon juice and a tablespoon of cold water. Slowly stir in a ladleful of the hot chicken stock, then add one or two more. Remove the pan from the heat, then pour in the egg mixture and stir well. Season to taste with salt and freshly ground black pepper and serve immediately. (Do not let the soup boil once the egg, lemon juice and stock mixture has been added, or it will curdle.)

Cappelletti in Broth

This soup is traditionally served in northern Italy on Santo Stefano (St Stephen's Day, the day after Christmas) and on New Year's Day as a welcome light change from all the special celebration food. Cappelletti are little stuffed pasta shapes that resemble hats.

SERVES FOUR

1.2 litres/2 pints/ 5 cups chicken stock

90–115g/3½–4oz/ 1 cup fresh or dried cappelletti

about 45ml/3 tbsp finely chopped fresh flat leaf parsley (optional)

about 30ml/2 tbsp freshly grated Parmesan cheese

1 Pour the chicken stock into a large pan and bring to the boil. Add a little seasoning to taste, then drop in the pasta.

2 Stir well and bring back to the boil. Lower the heat to a simmer and cook according to the instructions on the packet, until the pasta is *al dente*, that is, tender but still firm to the bite.

3 Swirl in the finely chopped fresh flat leaf parsley, if using, then taste and adjust the seasoning, if necessary. Ladle into four warmed soup plates, then sprinkle with the freshly grated Parmesan cheese and serve immediately.

COOK'S TIP

If you don't have home-made stock use two 300g/11oz cans of condensed beef consommé, adding water as instructed, or chilled commercial stock.

Tiny Pasta in Broth

This Italian soup is ideal for a light supper served with ciabatta bread and also makes a delicious first course for an *al fresco* supper. A wide variety of different types of *pastina* or soup pasta are available including stellette (stars), anellini (tiny thin rounds), risoni (rice-shaped) and farfalline (little butterflies). Choose just one shape or a combination of different varieties for an interesting result.

SERVES FOUR

1.2 litres/2 pints/ 5 cups beef stock

75g/3oz/¾ cup dried tiny soup pasta

2 pieces bottled roasted red (bell) pepper, about 50g/2oz

coarsely shaved Parmesan cheese

1 Bring the beef stock to the boil in a large pan. Add seasoning to taste, then drop in the dried soup pasta. Stir well and bring the stock back to the boil.

2 Reduce the heat so that the soup simmers and cook for 7–8 minutes, or according to the packet instructions, until the pasta is *al dente*, that is, tender but still firm to the bite.

3 Drain the pieces of roasted pepper and dice them finely. Place them in the base of four warmed soup plates. Taste the soup for seasoning before ladling it into the soup plates. Serve immediately, topped with shavings of Parmesan.

Linguine with Rocket

This fashionable first course is very quick and easy to make at home. Rocket has an excellent peppery flavour which combines beautifully with the rich, creamy tang of fresh Parmesan cheese. Fresh Parmesan keeps well in the refrigerator for up to a month – the dried variety is a very poor substitute and bears little resemblance to the real thing.

SERVES FOUR

1 Cook the pasta in a large pan of lightly salted boiling water according to the instructions on the packet, then drain thoroughly.

2 Heat about 60ml/4 tbsp of the olive oil in the pasta pan, then add the drained pasta, followed by the rocket. Toss over a medium to high heat for 1–2 minutes, or until the rocket is just wilted, then remove the pan from the heat.

3 Tip the pasta and rocket into a large, warmed bowl. Add half the freshly grated Parmesan and the remaining olive oil. Add a little salt and black pepper to taste.

4 Toss the mixture quickly to mix. Serve immediately, sprinkled with the remaining Parmesan.

350g/12oz fresh or dried linguine

120ml/4fl oz/½ cup extra virgin olive oil

1 large bunch rocket (arugula), about 150g/5oz, stalks removed, shredded or torn

75g/3oz/1 cup freshly grated Parmesan cheese

Tagliatelle with Vegetable Ribbons

Narrow strips of courgette and carrot mingle well with tagliatelle to resemble coloured pasta. Serve as a side dish, or sprinkle with freshly grated Parmesan cheese for a light appetizer or vegetarian main course. Garlic flavoured olive oil is used in this dish – flavoured oils such as rosemary, chilli or basil are widely available and are a quick way of adding flavour to pasta.

SERVES FOUR

2 large courgettes (zucchini)

2 large carrots

250g/9oz fresh egg tagliatelle

60ml/4 tbsp garlic flavoured olive oil

1 With a vegetable peeler, cut the courgettes and carrots into long thin ribbons. Bring a large pan of salted water to the boil, then add the courgette and carrot ribbons. Bring the water back to the boil and boil for 30 seconds, then drain and set aside.

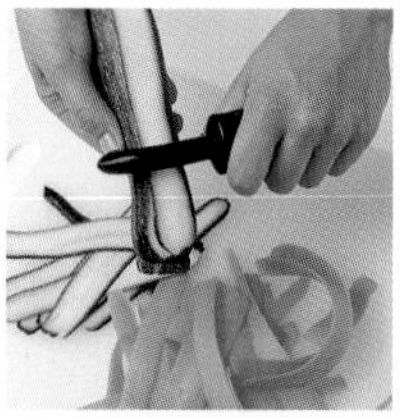

2 Cook the tagliatelle according to the instructions on the packet. Drain the pasta and return it to the pan. Add the vegetable ribbons, garlic flavoured oil and seasoning and toss over a medium to high heat until the pasta and vegetables are glistening with oil. Serve the pasta immediately.

Spaghetti with Lemon

This is the dish to make when you get home and find there's nothing to eat. If you keep spaghetti and olive oil in the store cupboard (pantry), and garlic and lemons in the vegetable rack, you can prepare this delicious meal in minutes. You can also add some freshly grated Parmesan cheese if you have some.

SERVES FOUR

350g/12oz dried spaghetti

90ml/6 tbsp extra virgin olive oil

juice of 1 large lemon

2 garlic cloves, cut into very thin slivers

1 Cook the pasta in a pan of salted boiling water according to the instructions on the packet, then drain well and return to the pan.

2 Pour the olive oil and lemon juice over the cooked pasta, sprinkle in the slivers of garlic and add seasoning to taste. Toss the pasta over a medium to high heat for 1–2 minutes. Serve immediately in four warmed bowls.

COOK'S TIP

Spaghetti is the best type of pasta for this recipe, because the olive oil and lemon juice cling to its long thin strands. If you are out of spaghetti, use another dried long pasta shape instead, such as spaghettini, linguine or tagliatelle.

Tofu and Pepper Kebabs

A simple coating of ground, dry-roasted peanuts pressed on to cubed tofu provides plenty of additional flavour along with the peppers. Use metal or bamboo skewers for the kebabs – if you use bamboo, then soak them in cold water for 30 minutes before using to prevent them from scorching during cooking. The kebabs can also be cooked on a barbecue, if you prefer.

SERVES FOUR

1 Pat the tofu dry on kitchen paper and then cut it into small cubes. Grind the peanuts in a blender or food processor and transfer to a plate. Turn the tofu cubes in the ground nuts to coat.

2 Preheat the grill (broiler) to moderate. Halve and seed the peppers, and cut them into large chunks. Thread the chunks of pepper on to four large skewers with the tofu cubes and place on a foil-lined grill rack.

3 Grill (broil) the kebabs, turning frequently, for 10 minutes, or until the peppers and peanuts are beginning to brown. Transfer the kebabs to plates and serve with the dipping sauce.

250g/9oz firm tofu

50g/2oz/½ cup dry-roasted peanuts

2 red and 2 green (bell) peppers

60ml/4 tbsp sweet chilli dipping sauce

Leek Fritters

These crispy fried morsels are best served at room temperature, with a good squeeze of lemon juice and a sprinkling of salt and freshly grated nutmeg. Matzo meal, a traditional Jewish ingredient, is used in these fritters: it is made from crumbled matzo, an unleavened bread, similar to water biscuits. Matzo meal is used in a similar way to breadcrumbs, which can also be used to make these fritters.

SERVES FOUR

4 large leeks, total weight about 1kg/ 2¼lb, thickly sliced

120–175ml/ 4–6fl oz/½–¾ cup coarse matzo meal

2 eggs, lightly beaten

olive or vegetable oil, for shallow frying

1 Cook the leeks in salted boiling water for 5 minutes, or until just tender and bright green. Drain well and leave to cool.

2 Chop the leeks coarsely. Put in a bowl and combine with the matzo meal, eggs and seasoning.

3 Heat 5mm/¼in oil in a frying pan. Using two tablespoons, carefully spoon the leek mixture into the hot oil. Cook over a medium-high heat until golden brown on the underside, then turn and cook the second side. Drain on kitchen paper. Add more oil if needed and heat before cooking more mixture.

Crisp Fried Whitebait

This must be one of the simplest of all classic fish dishes and it is absolutely delicious with lemon wedges and thinly sliced brown bread and butter. If you prefer, serve the whitebait with a simple lemon and herb dip – mix 150ml/¼ pint/⅔ cup natural (plain) yogurt with the rind of one lemon and 45ml/3 tbsp chopped fresh herbs. Serve chilled.

SERVES FOUR

oil, for deep-frying

150ml/¼ pint/⅔ cup milk

115g/4oz/1 cup plain (all-purpose) flour

450g/1lb whitebait

COOK'S TIP

Most whitebait are sold frozen. Thaw them before use and dry them thoroughly on kitchen paper before flouring.

1 Heat the oil in a large pan or deep-fryer. Put the milk in a shallow bowl and spoon the flour into a paper bag. Season the flour well with salt and pepper.

2 Dip a handful of the whitebait into the bowl of milk, drain them well, then pop them into the paper bag. Shake gently to coat them evenly in the seasoned flour, then transfer to a plate. Repeat until all the fish have been coated. This is the easiest method of flouring whitebait before frying, but don't add too many at once to the bag, or they will stick together.

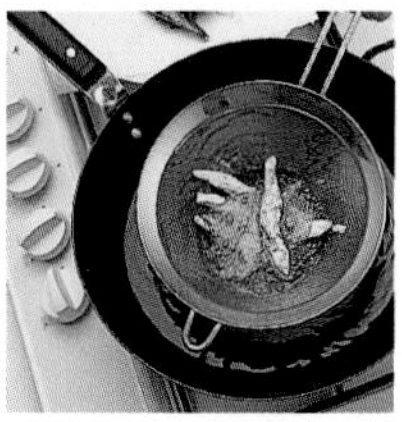

3 Heat the oil for deep-frying to 190°C/375°F or until a cube of stale bread, dropped into the oil, browns in about 20 seconds. Add a batch of whitebait, preferably in a frying basket, and deep-fry for 2–3 minutes, until crisp and golden brown. Drain and keep hot while you cook the rest. Serve very hot.

Crab and Cucumber Wraps

This dish is a modern twist on the ever-popular Chinese classic, crispy Peking duck with pancakes. In this quick and easy version, crisp, refreshing cucumber and full-flavoured dressed crab are delicious with spicy-sweet hoisin sauce in warm tortilla wraps. Serve the wraps as an appetizer for four people, or as a main course for two.

SERVES TWO

½ cucumber

1 medium dressed crab

4 small wheat tortillas

120ml/8 tbsp hoisin sauce

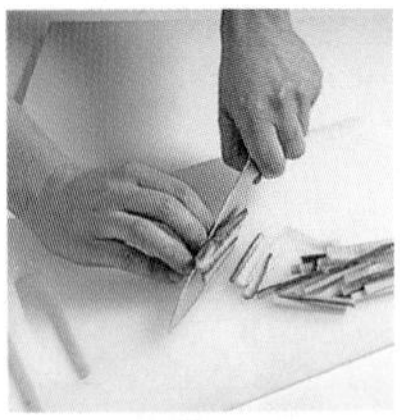

1 Cut the cucumber into small even-sized batons. Scoop the dressed crab into a small mixing bowl, add a little freshly ground black pepper and mix lightly to combine.

2 Heat the tortillas gently, one at a time, in a heavy frying pan until they begin to colour on each side.

3 Spread a tortilla with 30ml/2 tbsp hoisin sauce, then sprinkle with one-quarter of the cucumber. Arrange one-quarter of the seasoned crab meat down the centre of each tortilla and roll up. Repeat with the remaining ingredients. Serve immediately.

Pork Kebabs

The word kebab comes from Arabic and means on a skewer. Use pork fillet (tenderloin) for these kebabs because it is lean and tender, and cooks very quickly. They are good served with rice, or stuffed into warmed pitta bread with some shredded lettuce leaves.

SERVES FOUR

500g/1¼lb lean pork fillet (tenderloin)

8 large, thick spring onions (scallions), trimmed

120ml/4fl oz/½ cup barbecue sauce

1 lemon

1 Cut the pork into 2.5cm/1in cubes. Cut the spring onions into 2.5cm/1in long sticks.

2 Preheat the grill (broiler) to high. Oil the wire rack and spread out the pork cubes on it. Grill (broil) the pork until the juices drip, then dip the pieces in the barbecue sauce and put back on the grill. Grill for 30 seconds on each side, repeating the dipping process twice more. Set aside and keep warm.

3 Gently grill (broil) the spring onions until soft and slightly brown outside. Do not dip in the barbecue sauce. Thread about four pieces of pork and three spring onion pieces on to each of eight bamboo skewers.

4 Arrange the skewers on a platter. Cut the lemon into wedges and squeeze a little lemon juice over each skewer. Serve immediately, offering the remaining lemon wedges separately.

COOK'S TIP

If you are cooking the pork on a barbecue, soak the skewers overnight in water. This prevents them burning. Keep the skewer handles away from the fire and turn them frequently.

Main Meals

THE GOLDEN RULE FOR MAIN MEALS IN A HURRY IS THAT THE MOST SUCCESSFUL DISHES ARE OFTEN THE SIMPLEST. THE RECIPES IN THIS SECTION USE INTERESTING INGREDIENTS TO BRING NEW TASTE SENSATIONS TO YOUR TABLE. WHETHER YOU OPT FOR PASTA, A DELICIOUS CHILLI OR STEW, OR A DELECTABLE FISH OR MEAT DISH, YOU WILL BE GLAD YOU CHOSE THE EASY OPTION.

Fettucine all'Alfredo

This simple recipe was invented by a Roman restaurateur called Alfredo, who became famous for serving it with a gold fork and spoon. Today's busy cooks will find cartons of long-life cream invaluable for this type of recipe. If you can't get fettucine, any long ribbon-like pasta can be used in this dish – try tagliatelle or slightly wider pappardelle instead.

SERVES FOUR

50g/2oz/¼ cup butter

200ml/7fl oz/ scant 1 cup double (heavy) cream

50g/2oz/⅔ cup freshly grated Parmesan cheese, plus extra to serve

350g/12oz fresh fettucine

1 Melt the butter in a large pan. Add the cream and bring it to the boil. Simmer for 5 minutes, stirring constantly, then add the Parmesan cheese, with salt and freshly ground black pepper to taste, and turn off the heat under the pan.

2 Bring a large pan of salted water to the boil. Drop in the pasta all at once and quickly bring the water back to the boil, stirring occasionally. Cook the pasta for 2–3 minutes, or according to the instructions on the packet. Drain well.

3 Turn on the heat under the pan of cream to low, add the cooked pasta all at once and toss until it is thoroughly coated in the sauce. Taste the sauce for seasoning. Serve immediately, with extra grated Parmesan handed around separately.

Pansotti with Walnut Sauce

Walnuts and cream make a rich and luscious sauce for stuffed pasta, particularly the types filled with cheese and herbs. Serve this indulgent dish with warm walnut bread and a light, fruity white wine.

SERVES FOUR

90g/3½oz/scant 1 cup shelled walnuts

60ml/4 tbsp garlic-flavoured olive oil

120ml/4fl oz/½ cup double (heavy) cream

350g/12oz cheese and herb-filled pansotti or other stuffed pasta

1 Put the walnuts and garlic oil in a food processor and process to a paste, adding up to 120ml/4fl oz/½ cup warm water through the feeder tube to slacken the consistency. Spoon the mixture into a large bowl and add the cream. Beat well to mix, then season to taste with salt and black pepper.

2 Cook the pansotti or stuffed pasta in a large pan of salted boiling water for 4–5 minutes, or according to the instructions on the packet. Meanwhile, put the walnut sauce in a large warmed bowl and add a ladleful of the pasta cooking water to thin it.

3 Drain the pasta and tip it into the bowl of walnut sauce. Toss well, then serve immediately.

Farfalle with Tuna

Bought tomato sauce and canned tuna are endlessly versatile for making weekday suppers. A variety of herbs can be added to simple pasta dishes like this one – choose from basil, marjoram or oregano – and use fresh herbs, as the short cooking time does not allow the flavour of dried herbs to develop fully. Add a garnish of fresh oregano to this dish if you happen to have some.

SERVES FOUR

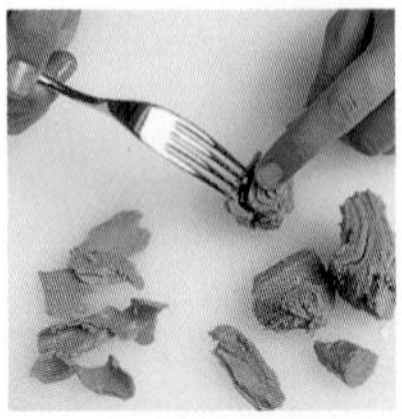

1 Cook the pasta in a large pan of lightly salted boiling water according to the instructions on the packet. Meanwhile, heat the tomato sauce in a separate pan and add the olives.

2 Drain the canned tuna and flake it with a fork. Add the tuna to the sauce with about 60ml/4 tbsp of the hot water used for cooking the pasta. Taste and adjust the seasoning.

3 Drain the pasta thoroughly and tip it into a large, warmed serving bowl. Pour the tuna sauce over the top and toss lightly to mix. Serve immediately.

400g/14oz/3½ cups dried farfalle

600ml/1 pint/2½ cups tomato sauce

175g/6oz can tuna in olive oil

8–10 pitted black olives, cut into rings

Mushroom Stroganoff

This creamy mixed mushroom sauce is ideal for a dinner party. Serve it with toasted buckwheat, brown rice or a mixture of wild rices and garnish with snipped chives. For best results, choose a variety of different mushrooms – wild mushrooms such as chanterelles, ceps and morels add a delicious flavour and texture to the stroganoff, as well as adding colour and producing a decorative appearance.

SERVES FOUR

25g/1oz/2 tbsp butter

900g/2lb mixed mushrooms, cut into bitesize pieces, including ⅔ button (white) mushrooms and ⅓ assorted wild or unusual mushrooms

350ml/12fl oz/ 1½ cups white wine sauce

250ml/8fl oz/1 cup sour cream

1 Melt the butter in a pan and quickly cook the mushrooms, in batches, over a high heat, until brown. Transfer the mushrooms to a bowl after cooking each batch.

2 Add the sauce to the juices remaining in the pan and bring to the boil, stirring. Reduce the heat and replace the mushrooms with any juices from the bowl. Stir well and heat for a few seconds, then remove from the heat.

3 Stir the sour cream into the cooked mushroom mixture and season to taste with salt and lots of freshly ground black pepper. Heat through gently for a few seconds, if necessary, then transfer to warm plates and serve immediately.

Mixed Bean and Tomato Chilli

Here, mixed beans, fiery red chilli and plenty of freshly chopped coriander are simmered in a tomato sauce to make a delicious vegetarian chilli. Always a popular dish, chilli can be served with a variety of accompaniments – choose from baked potatoes, baked rice, crusty bread or tortillas. Garnish with slices of tomato, chopped celery or sweet (bell) pepper and top with natural (plain) yogurt.

SERVES FOUR

1 Pour the tomato sauce and mixed beans into a pan. Seed and thinly slice the chilli, then add it to the pan. Reserve a little of the coriander, chop the remainder and add it to the pan.

2 Bring the mixture to the boil, reduce the heat, cover and simmer gently for 10 minutes. Stir the mixture occasionally and add a dash of water if the sauce starts to dry out.

3 Ladle the chilli into warmed individual serving bowls and top with a spoonful of yogurt to serve.

400g/14oz jar tomato and herb sauce

2 x 400g/14oz cans mixed beans, drained and rinsed

1 fresh red chilli

large handful of fresh coriander (cilantro)

Prawn and New Potato Stew

New potatoes with plenty of flavour, such as Jersey Royals, Maris Piper or Nicola, are essential for this effortless stew. Use a good quality jar of tomato and chilli sauce; there are now plenty available in the supermarkets. For a really easy supper dish, serve with warm, crusty bread to mop up the delicious sauce, and a mixed green salad.

SERVES FOUR

675g/1½lb small new potatoes, cooked

15g/½oz/½ cup fresh coriander (cilantro)

350g/12oz jar tomato and chilli sauce

300g/11oz cooked peeled prawns (shrimp), thawed and drained if frozen

1 Cook the potatoes in lightly salted, boiling water until tender. Drain and return to the pan.

2 Finely chop half the coriander and add to the pan with the tomato and chilli sauce and 90ml/6 tbsp water. Bring to the boil, reduce the heat, cover and simmer gently for 5 minutes.

3 Stir in the prawns and heat briefly until they are warmed through. Do not overheat the prawns or they will quickly shrivel, becoming tough and tasteless. Spoon into shallow bowls and serve sprinkled with the remaining coriander, torn into pieces.

Scallops with Fennel and Bacon

This dish is a delicious combination of succulent scallops and crispy bacon, served on a bed of tender fennel and melting mascarpone. If you can't get large scallops (known as king scallops), buy the smaller queen scallops and serve a dozen per person. If you buy scallops in the shell, wash and keep the pretty fan-shaped shells for serving a range of fish dishes.

SERVES TWO

2 small fennel bulbs

130g/4½oz/ generous ½ cup mascarpone cheese

8 large scallops, shelled

75g/3oz thin smoked streaky (fatty) bacon rashers (strips)

1 Trim, halve and slice the fennel, reserving and chopping any feathery tops. Blanch the slices in boiling water for about 3 minutes, until softened, then drain.

2 Preheat the grill (broiler) to moderate. Place the fennel in a shallow flameproof dish and season with salt and pepper. Dot with the mascarpone and grill (broil) for about 5 minutes, until the cheese has melted and the fennel is lightly browned.

3 Meanwhile, pat the scallops dry on kitchen paper and season lightly. Cook the bacon in a large, heavy frying pan, until crisp and golden, turning once. Drain and keep warm. Fry the scallops in the bacon fat for 1–2 minutes on each side, until cooked through.

4 Transfer the fennel to serving plates and crumble or snip the bacon into bite size pieces over the top. Pile the scallops on the bacon and sprinkle with any reserved fennel tops.

Poached Fish in Spicy Tomato Sauce

A selection of white fish fillets are used in this Middle-Eastern dish – cod, haddock, hake or halibut are all good. Serve the fish with flat breads, such as pitta, and a spicy tomato relish. It is also good with couscous or rice and a green salad with a refreshing lemon juice dressing.

SERVES EIGHT

1 Heat the tomato sauce with the harissa and coriander in a large pan. Add seasoning to taste and bring to the boil.

2 Remove the pan from the heat and add the fish to the hot sauce. Return to the heat and bring the sauce to the boil again. Reduce the heat and simmer very gently for about 5 minutes, or until the fish is tender. (Test with a fork: if the flesh flakes easily, then it is cooked.)

3 Taste the sauce and adjust the seasoning, adding more harissa if necessary. Serve hot or warm.

600ml/1 pint/2½ cups fresh tomato sauce

2.5–5ml/½–1 tsp harissa

60ml/4 tbsp chopped fresh coriander (cilantro) leaves

1.5kg/3¼lb mixed white fish fillets, cut into chunks

COOK'S TIP

Harissa is a chilli paste spiced with cumin, garlic and coriander. It is fiery and should be used with care until you are familiar with the flavour. Start by adding a small amount and then add more after tasting the sauce.

Lamb Steaks with Redcurrant Glaze

This classic, simple dish is absolutely delicious and is an excellent, quick recipe for cooking on the barbecue. The tangy flavour of redcurrants is a traditional accompaniment to lamb. It is good served with new potatoes and fresh garden peas tossed in butter.

SERVES FOUR

4 large fresh rosemary sprigs

4 lamb leg steaks

75ml/5 tbsp redcurrant jelly

30ml/2 tbsp raspberry or red wine vinegar

1 Reserve the tips of the rosemary and finely chop the remaining leaves. Rub the chopped rosemary, salt and pepper all over the lamb.

2 Preheat the grill (broiler). Heat the redcurrant jelly gently in a small pan with 30ml/2 tbsp water and a little seasoning. Stir in the vinegar.

3 Place the lamb steaks on a foil-lined grill (broiler) rack and brush with a little of the redcurrant glaze. Cook under the grill for about 5 minutes on each side, until deep golden, brushing frequently with more redcurrant glaze.

4 Transfer the lamb to warmed plates. Tip any juices from the foil into the remaining glaze and heat through gently. Pour the glaze over the lamb and serve, garnished with the reserved rosemary sprigs.

Steak with Warm Tomato Salsa

A refreshing, tangy salsa of tomatoes, spring onions and balsamic vinegar makes a colourful topping for chunky, pan-fried steaks. Choose rump, sirloin or fillet – whichever is your favourite – and if you do not have a non-stick pan, grill the steak instead for the same length of time. Serve with potato wedges and a mixed leaf salad with a mustard dressing.

SERVES TWO

2 steaks, about 2cm/ ¾in thick

4 large plum tomatoes

2 spring onions (scallions)

30ml/2 tbsp balsamic vinegar

1 Trim any excess fat from the steaks, then season on both sides with salt and pepper. Heat a non-stick frying pan and cook the steaks for about 3 minutes on each side for medium rare. Cook for a little longer if you like your steak well cooked.

2 Meanwhile, put the tomatoes in a heatproof bowl, cover with boiling water and leave for 1–2 minutes, until the skins start to split. Drain and peel the tomatoes, then halve them and scoop out the seeds. Dice the tomato flesh. Thinly slice the spring onions.

3 Transfer the steaks to plates and keep warm. Add the vegetables, balsamic vinegar, 30ml/2 tbsp water and a little seasoning to the cooking juices in the pan and stir briefly until warm, scraping up any meat residue. Spoon the salsa over the steaks to serve.

Side Dishes and Accompaniments

A FEW CAREFULLY-CHOSEN INGREDIENTS CAN BE BROUGHT TOGETHER TO CREATE MOUTHWATERING SIDE DISHES AND ACCOMPANIMENTS THAT WILL COMPLEMENT AND ENHANCE ANY MAIN DISH. THIS COLLECTION OF TASTY AND COLOURFUL COMBINATIONS OF VEGETABLES MAKES HEALTHY EATING A TEMPTING TREAT.

Watermelon and Feta Salad

The combination of sweet watermelon with salty feta cheese is inspired by Turkish tradition. The salad may be served plain and light, on a leafy base, or with a herbed vinaigrette dressing drizzled over. It is perfect served as an appetizer. Feta cheese is salty because it is preserved in brine – but the salt is not supposed to overpower the taste of the cheese.

SERVES FOUR

4 slices watermelon, chilled

130g/4½oz feta cheese, preferably sheep's milk feta, cut into bitesize pieces

handful of mixed seeds, such as lightly toasted pumpkin seeds and sunflower seeds

10–15 black olives

1 Cut the rind off the watermelon and remove as many seeds as possible. Cut the flesh into triangular-shaped chunks.

2 Mix the watermelon, feta cheese, mixed seeds and black olives. Cover and chill the salad before serving.

COOK'S TIP

The best choice of olives for this recipe are plump black Mediterranean ones, such as kalamata, other shiny, brined varieties or dry-cured black olives.

Beetroot with Fresh Mint

This simple and decorative beetroot salad can be served as part of a selection of salads, as an appetizer, or as an accompaniment to grilled or roasted pork or lamb. Balsamic vinegar is a rich, dark vinegar with a mellow, deep flavour. It can be used to dress a variety of salad ingredients and is particularly good drizzled over a tomato and basil salad.

SERVES FOUR

4–6 cooked beetroot (beet)

15–30ml/1–2 tbsp balsamic vinegar

30ml/2 tbsp olive oil

1 bunch fresh mint, leaves stripped and thinly shredded

1 Slice the beetroot or cut into even-size dice with a sharp knife. Put the beetroot in a bowl. Add the balsamic vinegar, olive oil and a pinch of salt and toss together to combine.

2 Add half the thinly shredded fresh mint to the salad and toss lightly until thoroughly combined. Place the salad in the refrigerator and chill until ready to serve. Serve garnished with the remaining thinly shredded mint leaves.

EXTRAS

To make Tunisian beetroot, add a little harissa to taste and substitute chopped fresh coriander (cilantro) for the shredded mint.

Moroccan Date, Orange and Carrot Salad

Take exotic fresh dates and marry them with everyday ingredients, such as carrots and oranges, to make this deliciously different salad. The salad looks very pretty arranged on a base of sweet Little Gem (Bibb) lettuce leaves. This fruity salad is excellent served with chargrilled lamb steaks, or with skewered lamb.

SERVES FOUR

3 carrots

3 oranges

115g/4oz fresh dates, stoned (pitted) and cut lengthways into eighths

25g/1oz/¼ cup toasted whole almonds, chopped

1 Grate the carrots and place in a mound in a serving dish, or on four individual plates.

2 Peel and segment two of the oranges and arrange the orange segments around the carrot. Season with salt and freshly ground black pepper. Pile the dates on top, then sprinkle with the chopped, toasted almonds.

3 Squeeze the juice from the remaining orange and sprinkle it over the salad. Chill in the refrigerator for an hour before serving.

Halloumi and Grape Salad

Firm and salty halloumi cheese is a great standby ingredient for turning a simple salad into a special dish. In this recipe it is tossed with sweet, juicy grapes, which complement its flavour and texture. Fresh young thyme leaves and dill taste especially good mixed with the salad. Serve with a crusty walnut or sun-dried tomato bread for a light lunch.

SERVES FOUR

150g/5oz mixed salad leaves and tender fresh herb sprigs

175g/6oz mixed seedless green and black grapes

250g/9oz halloumi cheese

75ml/5 tbsp oil and lemon juice or vinegar dressing

1 Toss together the salad leaves and fresh herb sprigs and the green and black grapes, then transfer to a large serving plate.

2 Thinly slice the halloumi cheese. Heat a large non-stick frying pan. Add the sliced halloumi cheese and cook briefly until it just starts to turn golden brown on the underside. Turn the cheese with a fish slice or metal spatula and cook the other side until it is golden brown.

3 Arrange the fried cheese over the salad on the plate. Pour over the oil and lemon juice or vinegar dressing and serve immediately while the cheese is still hot.

Moroccan Carrot Salad

In this intriguing salad from North Africa, the carrots are lightly cooked before being tossed in a cumin and coriander vinaigrette. Cumin is widely used in Indian and Mexican cooking, as well as North African cuisines. It has a strong and spicy aroma and a warm pungent flavour that goes particularly well with root vegetables. This salad is a perfect accompaniment for both everyday or special meals.

SERVES FOUR TO SIX

3–4 carrots, thinly sliced

1.5ml/¼ tsp ground cumin, or to taste

60ml/4 tbsp garlic-flavoured oil and vinegar dressing

30ml/2 tbsp chopped fresh coriander (cilantro) leaves or a mixture of coriander and parsley

1 Cook the thinly sliced carrots by either steaming or boiling in lightly salted water until they are just tender but not soft. Drain the carrots, leave for a few minutes to dry and cool, then put into a mixing bowl.

2 Add the cumin, garlic dressing and herbs. Season to taste and chill well before serving. Check the seasoning just before serving and add more ground cumin, salt or black pepper, if required.

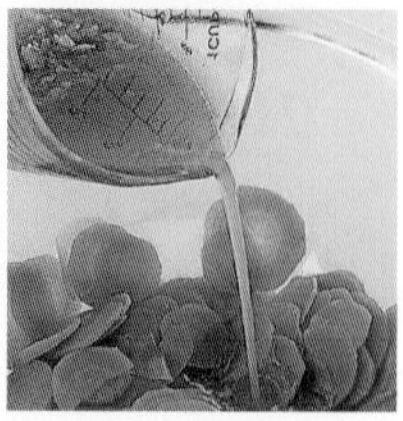

Turnip Salad in Sour Cream

Usually served cooked, raw young tender turnips have a tangy, slightly peppery flavour. Serve this as an accompaniment for grilled poultry or meat. It is also delicious as a light appetizer, garnished with parsley and paprika, and served with warmed flat breads such as pitta or naan. Garnish the salad with fresh flat leaf parsley and paprika, if you like.

SERVES FOUR

2–4 young, tender turnips, peeled

¼–½ onion, finely chopped

2–3 drops white wine vinegar, or to taste

60–90ml/4–6 tbsp sour cream

1 Thinly slice or coarsely grate the turnips. Alternatively, thinly slice half the turnips and grate the remaining half. Put in a bowl.

2 Add the onion and vinegar and season to taste with salt and plenty of freshly ground black pepper. Toss together, then stir in the sour cream. Chill well before serving.

VARIATIONS

Large white radishes can be used instead of turnips and crème fraîche can be substituted for the sour cream. The salad is good with a selection of salads and cold dishes for a light lunch or long and leisurely supper.

Warm Chorizo and Spinach Salad

Spanish chorizo sausage contributes an intense spiciness to any ingredient with which it is cooked. In this hearty warm salad, spinach has sufficient flavour to compete with the chorizo. Watercress or rocket (arugula) could be used instead of the spinach, if you prefer. For an added dimension use a flavoured olive oil – rosemary, garlic or chilli oil would work perfectly. Serve the salad with warm crusty bread to soak up all the delicious cooking juices.

SERVES FOUR

225g/8oz baby spinach leaves

90ml/6 tbsp extra virgin olive oil

150g/5oz chorizo sausage, very thinly sliced

30ml/2 tbsp sherry vinegar

1 Discard any tough stalks from the spinach. Pour the oil into a large frying pan and add the sausage. Cook gently for 3 minutes, until the sausage slices start to shrivel slightly and colour.

2 Add the spinach leaves and remove the pan from the heat. Toss the spinach in the warm oil until it just starts to wilt. Add the sherry vinegar and a little seasoning. Toss the ingredients briefly, then serve immediately, while still warm.

Cauliflower with Garlic Crumbs

This simple dish makes a great accompaniment to any meat or fish dish. When buying cauliflower look for creamy white coloured florets with the inner green leaves curled round the flower. Discard cauliflowers with discoloured patches or yellow leaves. As an alternative, try using broccoli florets instead of the cauliflower. Broccoli should have a fresh appearance: avoid yellowing specimens and those that feel soft or are wilting.

SERVES FOUR TO SIX

1 large cauliflower, cut into bitesize florets

90–120ml/6–8 tbsp olive or vegetable oil

130g/4½oz/2¼ cups dry white or wholemeal (whole-wheat) breadcrumbs

3–5 garlic cloves, thinly sliced or chopped

1 Steam or boil the cauliflower in salted water until just tender. Drain and leave to cool.

2 Heat 60–75ml/4–5 tbsp of the olive or vegetable oil in a pan, add the breadcrumbs and cook over a medium heat, tossing and turning, until browned and crisp. Add the garlic, turn once or twice, then remove from the pan and set aside.

3 Heat the remaining oil in the pan, then add the cauliflower, mashing and breaking it up a little as it lightly browns in the oil. (Do not overcook but just cook until lightly browned.)

4 Add the garlic breadcrumbs to the pan and cook, stirring, until well combined, with some of the cauliflower still holding its shape. Season and serve hot or warm.

COOK'S TIP

Serve this wonderful, garlicky cauliflower dish as they do in Italy, with cooked pasta, such as spaghetti or rigatoni.

Caramelized Shallots

Sweet, golden shallots are good with all sorts of main dishes, including poultry or meat. Shallots have a less distinctive aroma than common onions and a milder flavour; they are also considered to be easier to digest. These caramelized shallots are also excellent with braised or roasted chestnuts, carrots or chunks of butternut squash. You may like to garnish the shallots with sprigs of fresh thyme before serving.

SERVES FOUR TO SIX

1 Heat the butter or oil in a large frying pan and add the shallots or onions in a single layer. Cook gently, turning occasionally, until they are lightly browned.

2 Sprinkle the sugar over the shallots and cook gently, turning the shallots in the juices, until the sugar begins to caramelize. Add the wine or port and let the mixture bubble for 4–5 minutes.

3 Add 150ml/¼ pint/⅔ cup water and seasoning. Cover and cook for 5 minutes, then remove the lid and cook until the liquid evaporates and the shallots are tender and glazed. Adjust the seasoning before serving.

50g/2oz/¼ cup butter or 60ml/4 tbsp olive oil

500g/1¼lb shallots or small onions, peeled with root ends intact

15ml/1 tbsp golden caster (superfine) sugar

30ml/2 tbsp red or white wine or port

Braised Lettuce and Peas with Spring Onions

This light vegetable dish is based on the classic French method of braising peas with lettuce and spring onions in butter, and is delicious served with simply grilled fish or roast or grilled duck. A sprinkling of chopped fresh mint makes a fresh, flavoursome and extremely pretty garnish. Other legumes such as broad (fava) beans, mangetouts (snow peas) and sugar snaps can be used instead of peas to create a delicious variation.

SERVES FOUR

50g/2oz/¼ cup butter

4 Little Gem (Bibb) lettuces, halved lengthways

2 bunches spring onions (scallions), trimmed

400g/14oz shelled peas (about 1kg/2¼lb in pods)

1 Melt half the butter in a wide, heavy pan over a low heat. Add the lettuces and spring onions.

2 Turn the vegetables in the butter, then sprinkle in salt and plenty of freshly ground black pepper. Cover, and cook the vegetables very gently for 5 minutes, stirring once.

3 Add the peas and turn them in the buttery juices. Pour in 120ml/4fl oz/½ cup water, then cover and cook over a gentle heat for a further 5 minutes. Uncover and increase the heat to reduce the liquid to a few tablespoons.

4 Stir in the remaining butter and adjust the seasoning. Transfer to a warmed serving dish and serve immediately.

EXTRAS

- *Braise about 250g/9oz baby carrots with the lettuce.*
- *Cook 115g/4oz chopped smoked bacon or pancetta in the butter. Use one bunch of spring onions (scallions) and stir in some chopped parsley.*

Hot Mango Salsa

For sweet, tangy results, select a really juicy, ripe mango for this salsa – it is not worth making the salsa with a firm, unripe mango as it will not taste as good as it should. Keep an unripe mango in the fruit bowl for a few days until it has ripened. This fruity salsa is a delicious accompaniment to chargrilled or barbecued chicken or fish.

SERVES FOUR TO SIX

1 To prepare the mango, cut the flesh off on either side of the flat stone (pit). Peel and finely dice the mango halves and cut off and chop the flesh that still clings to the stone.

2 Finely grate the lime rind and squeeze the juice. Seed and finely shred the fresh red chilli.

3 Finely chop the onion and mix it in a bowl with the mango, lime rind, 15ml/1 tbsp lime juice, the chilli and a little salt. Cover and chill until ready to serve.

1 medium ripe mango

1 lime

1 large mild fresh red chilli

½ small red onion

Yellow Pepper and Coriander Relish

Relishes are quick and easy to make and they are delicious with cold meats and cheese or as a sandwich filler. Here the ingredients are lightly cooked, then processed to a chunky consistency. Red or orange (bell) peppers will work just as well as yellow as they all have a sweet flavour. Don't use green peppers though, because they are not sweet.

SERVES FOUR TO SIX

3 large yellow (bell) peppers

45ml/3 tbsp sesame oil

1 large mild fresh red chilli

small handful of fresh coriander (cilantro)

1 Seed and coarsely chop the peppers. Heat the oil in a frying pan and gently cook the peppers, stirring frequently, for 8–10 minutes, until lightly coloured.

2 Meanwhile, seed the chilli and slice it as thinly as possible. Transfer the peppers and cooking juices to a food processor and process lightly until chopped. Transfer half the peppers to a bowl. Using a sharp knife, chop the fresh coriander, then add to the food processor and process briefly.

3 Tip the contents of the food processor into the bowl with the rest of the peppers and add the chilli and salt. Mix well, cover and chill until ready to serve.

COOK'S TIP

Other flavoured oils, such as lemon- or garlic-infused oil, can be used in place of the sesame oil. The relish can be stored in an airtight container in the refrigerator for several days.

Harissa

This simplified version of harissa – the classic spicy North African sauce – is extremely quick to make. It can be served as a dip with wedges of Middle Eastern flat bread, as a condiment with couscous and other North African dishes, or as a flavouring to spice up meat and vegetable stews. This basic spice blend goes very well with other aromatic herbs and spices so you can vary the flavour by adding chopped fresh coriander (cilantro) or a pinch of caraway seeds along with the lemon juice, if you like.

SERVES FOUR TO SIX

1 Put the paprika, cayenne pepper, ground cumin and 250ml/8fl oz/1 cup water in a large, heavy pan and season with salt to taste.

2 Bring the spice mixture to the boil, then immediately remove the pan from the heat.

3 Stir in the lemon juice to taste and allow to cool completely before serving or using.

45ml/3 tbsp paprika

2.5–5ml/½–1 tsp cayenne pepper

1.5ml/¼ tsp ground cumin

juice of ¼–½ lemon

Roasted Garlic Sauce

A roasted garlic sauce has plenty of robust flavour without the harshness of some uncooked garlic sauces and dressings. This one keeps well in the refrigerator for several days. Serve it as an accompaniment to barbecued burgers or sausages, grilled steaks, lamb chops or pork steaks – the possibilities are endless.

SERVES SIX TO EIGHT

6 large heads of garlic, cooked

120ml/4fl oz/½ cup extra virgin olive oil

2 thick slices white bread, about 90g/3½oz

30–45ml/2–3 tbsp lemon juice

1 To cook the garlic: Preheat the oven to 200°C/400°F/Gas 6. Slice the tops off the garlic and place the bulbs on a sheet of foil. Spoon over 30ml/2 tbsp of the oil and sprinkle with salt. Wrap the foil over the garlic and bake for 1 hour, until soft. Open out the foil and leave the garlic to cool.

2 Discard the crusts from the bread. Soak the bread in water for 1 minute, then squeeze dry and place in a food processor. Squeeze the garlic flesh into the processor. Process to a smooth paste.

3 Add 30ml/2 tbsp lemon juice with a little salt and pepper. With the machine running, gradually add the remaining oil in a thin stream to make a smooth paste. Check the seasoning, adding more lemon juice if needed. Turn into a bowl, cover and chill until required.

Pastries and Desserts

ALL THE RECIPES IN THIS CHAPTER HAVE AN ELEGANT SIMPLICITY THAT GUARANTEES SUCCESS EVEN WITH THE MOST SOPHISTICATED DINNER GUESTS. MAKE A DELICIOUS SORBET OR WATER ICE IN ADVANCE – THEY ARE EASY TO PREPARE AND MAKE A PERFECT AFTER-DINNER TREAT.

Cinnamon Pinwheels

These impressive sweet pastries go well with tea or coffee or as an accompaniment to ice cream and creamy desserts. If you find they turn soft during storage, re-crisp them briefly in the oven. Cinnamon is widely used in both sweet and savoury cooking: here ground cinnamon is used but it is also available as woody sticks. It has a delicious fragrant aroma and gives these simple-to-make pinwheels a warm spicy flavour.

MAKES TWENTY TO TWENTY-FOUR

50g/2oz/¼ cup caster (superfine) sugar, plus a little extra for sprinkling

10ml/2 tsp ground cinnamon

250g/9oz puff pastry

beaten egg, to glaze

1 Preheat the oven to 220°C/425°F/Gas 7. Grease a large baking sheet. Mix the sugar with the cinnamon in a small bowl.

2 Roll out the pastry on a lightly floured surface to a 20cm/8in square and sprinkle with half the sugar mixture. Roll out the pastry to a 25cm/10in square so that the sugar is pressed into it.

3 Brush with the beaten egg and then sprinkle with the remaining sugar mixture. Loosely roll up the pastry into a log, brushing the end of the pastry with a little more egg to secure the edge in place.

4 Using a sharp knife, cut the log into thin slices and transfer them to the prepared baking sheet. Bake for 10 minutes, until golden and crisp. Sprinkle with more sugar and transfer to a wire rack to cool.

Summer Fruit Brioche

Scooped-out, individual brioches make perfect containers for the fruity filling in this stylish, but simple dessert. If small brioches are not available, serve the fruit on slices cut from a large brioche. Any summer fruits can be used in this dessert – try raspberries, sliced peaches, nectarines, apricots, or pitted cherries. Serve with single (light) cream poured over.

SERVES FOUR

4 individual brioches

300g/11oz/ 2½ cups small ripe strawberries, halved

30ml/2 tbsp caster (superfine) sugar

115g/4oz/⅔ cup raspberries

1 Preheat the grill (broiler). Slice the tops off the brioches and use a teaspoon to scoop out their centres, leaving a 1 cm/½in thick case. Lightly toast them, turning once and watching them carefully, as they will brown very quickly.

2 Put the strawberries in a pan with the sugar and add 60ml/4 tbsp water. Heat very gently for about 1 minute, until the strawberries are softened but still keep their shape. Remove the pan from the heat, stir in the raspberries and leave to cool.

3 Place the brioches on plates and pile the fruit mixture into them. Add plenty of juice to saturate the brioches and allow it to flood the plates. Place any extra fruit on the plates.

Tropical Scented Fruit Salad

With its special colour and exotic flavour, this fresh fruit salad is perfect after a rich, heavy meal. For fabulous flavour and colour, try using three small blood oranges and three ordinary oranges. Other fruit that can be added include pears, kiwi fruit and bananas. Serve the fruit salad with whipping cream flavoured with 15g/½oz finely chopped drained preserved stem ginger.

SERVES FOUR TO SIX

1 Put the hulled and halved strawberries and peeled and segmented oranges into a serving bowl. Halve the passion fruit and using a teaspoon scoop the flesh into the bowl.

2 Pour the wine over the fruit and toss gently. Cover and chill in the refrigerator until ready to serve.

350–400g/12–14oz/3–3½ cups strawberries, hulled and halved

6 oranges, peeled and segmented

1–2 passion fruit

120ml/4fl oz/½ cup medium dry or sweet white wine

Summer Berries in Sabayon Glaze

This luxurious combination of summer berries under a light and fluffy liqueur sauce is lightly grilled to form a crisp, caramelized topping. Fresh or frozen berries can be used in this dessert. If you use frozen berries, defrost them in a sieve over a bowl to allow the juices to drip. Stir a little juice into the fruit before dividing among the dishes.

SERVES FOUR

1 Arrange the mixed summer berries or soft fruit in four individual flameproof dishes. Preheat the grill (broiler).

2 Whisk the yolks in a large bowl with the sugar and liqueur or wine. Place over a pan of hot water and whisk constantly until the mixture is thick, fluffy and pale.

3 Pour equal quantities of the yolk mixture into each dish. Place under the grill for 1–2 minutes, until just turning brown. Add an extra splash of liqueur, if you like, and serve immediately.

450g/1lb/4 cups mixed summer berries, or soft fruit

4 egg yolks

50g/2oz/¼ cup vanilla sugar or caster (superfine) sugar

120ml/4fl oz/½ cup liqueur, such as Cointreau or Kirsch, or a white dessert wine

Zabaglione

Light as air and wonderfully heady, this warm, wine egg custard is a much-loved Italian dessert. Traditionally made with Sicilian Marsala, other fortified wines such as Madeira or sweet sherry can be used.

SERVES FOUR

4 egg yolks

50g/2oz/¼ cup caster (superfine) sugar

60ml/4 tbsp Marsala, Madeira or sweet sherry

amaretti biscuits, to serve

1 Place the egg yolks and sugar in a large heatproof bowl and whisk with an electric beater until the mixture is pale and thick.

2 Gradually add the Marsala, Madeira or sweet sherry to the egg mixture, 15ml/1 tbsp at a time, whisking well after each addition.

3 Place the bowl over a pan of gently simmering water and whisk for 5–7 minutes, until thick: when the beaters are lifted, they should leave a thick trail on the surface of the mixture. Do not be tempted to give up when beating the mixture, as the zabaglione will be too runny and will be likely to separate if it is underbeaten.

4 Pour into four warmed, stemmed glasses and serve immediately, with amaretti for dipping.

EXTRAS

Marinate chopped strawberries in a little extra Marsala, Madeira or sweet sherry for an hour or so. Sweeten with sugar, if you like, and spoon into glasses before you add the zabaglione.

Whisked Chocolate Custard

Once you've tasted this sensuous dessert, you'll never regard cocoa in quite the same way again. The custard can be dusted with icing (confectioners') sugar instead of extra cocoa, if you like. Serve with mini amaretti or other small, crisp biscuits (cookies).

SERVES SIX

6 egg yolks

150g/5oz/¾ cup caster (superfine) sugar

45ml/3 tbsp (unsweetened) cocoa powder, plus extra for dusting

200ml/7fl oz/scant 1 cup Marsala

1 Prepare a pan of simmering water and a heatproof bowl to fit on top. Place the egg yolks and sugar in the bowl and whisk, off the heat, until the mixture is pale and all the sugar has dissolved.

2 Add the cocoa and Marsala, then place the bowl over the simmering water. Beat with a hand-held electric mixer until the mixture is smooth, thick and foamy.

3 Pour quickly into tall glasses, dust lightly with cocoa and serve immediately, with amaretti or other dessert biscuits, if liked.

Blackcurrant Sorbet

Wonderfully sharp and bursting with flavour, blackcurrants make a really fabulous sorbet. Blackcurrants are more acidic than white or redcurrants and are very rarely eaten raw. Taste the mixture after adding the syrup, and if you find it a little too tart, add a little more sugar before freezing.

SERVES SIX

500g/1¼lb/5 cups blackcurrants, trimmed, plus extra to decorate

150g/5oz/¾ cup caster (superfine) sugar

1 egg white

1 Put the blackcurrants in a pan and add 150ml/¼ pint/⅔ cup water. Cover the pan and simmer for 5 minutes, or until the fruit is soft. Cool, then process to a purée in a food processor or blender.

2 Set a large sieve over a bowl, pour the purée into the sieve, then press it through the mesh with the back of a spoon to form a smooth liquid.

3 Pour 200ml/7fl oz/scant 1 cup water into a clean pan. Add the sugar and bring to the boil, stirring until the sugar has dissolved. Pour the syrup into a bowl. Cool, then chill.

4 Mix the blackcurrant purée and sugar syrup together. Spoon into a freezerproof container and freeze until mushy. Lightly whisk the egg white until just frothy. Process the sorbet (sherbet) in a food processor until smooth, then return it to the container and stir in the egg white. Freeze for 4 hours, or until firm.

5 Transfer the sorbet to the refrigerator about 15 minutes before serving. Serve in scoops, decorated with the blackcurrant sprigs.

Damson Water Ice

Perfectly ripe damsons are sharp and full of flavour – if you can't find damsons, use another deep-red variety of plum or extra-juicy Victoria plums. To add an extra, nutty flavour to this mouthwatering ice, serve sprinkled with finely chopped toasted almonds.

SERVES SIX

500g/1¼ lb ripe damsons, washed

150g/5oz/¾ cup caster (superfine) sugar

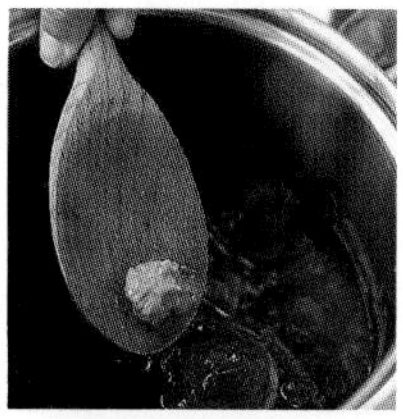

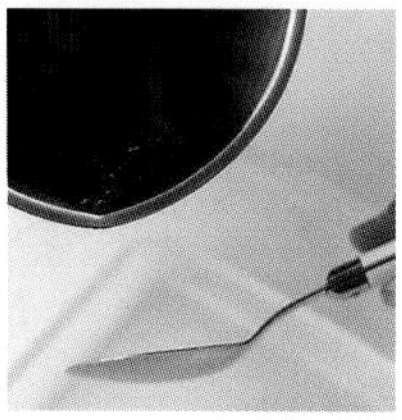

1 Put the damsons into a pan and add 150ml/¼ pint/⅔ cup water. Cover and simmer gently for 10 minutes, or until the damsons are tender.

2 Pour 300ml/½ pint/1¼ cups water into a second pan. Add the sugar and bring to the boil, stirring until the sugar has dissolved. Pour the syrup into a bowl, leave to cool, then chill.

3 Break up the cooked damsons in the pan with a wooden spoon and scoop out any free stones (pits). Pour the fruit and juices into a large sieve set over a bowl. Press the fruit through the sieve and discard the skins and any remaining stones from the sieve.

4 Pour the damson purée into a shallow plastic container. Stir in the syrup and freeze for 6 hours, beating once or twice to break up the ice crystals.

5 Spoon into tall serving glasses or dishes and serve the water ice with wafers.

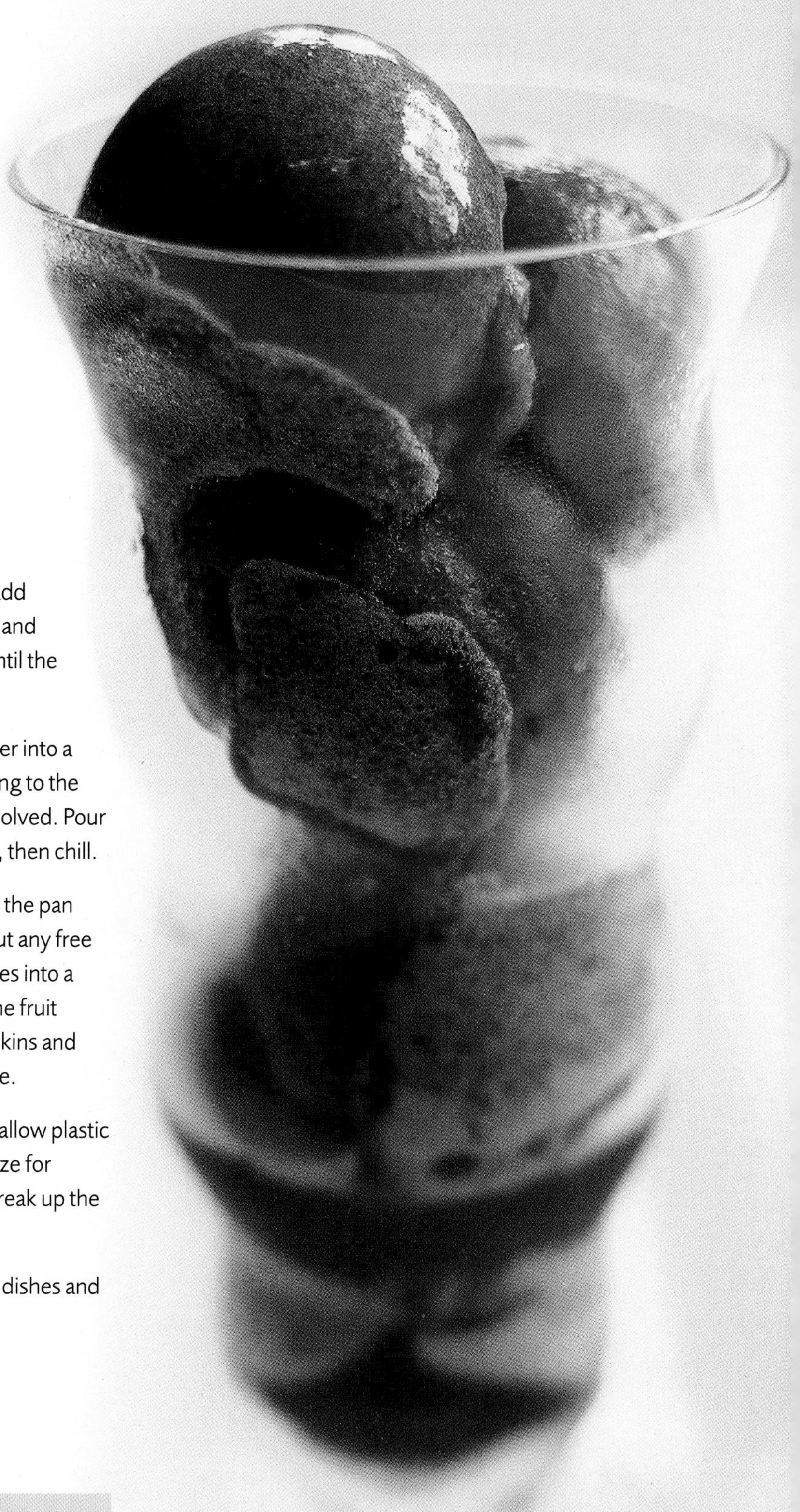

VARIATION

Apricot water ice can be made in exactly the same way. Flavour the water ice with a little lemon or orange rind or add a broken cinnamon stick to the pan when poaching the fruit. Serve garnished with sprigs of mint or nasturtium flowers.

Soft Fruit and Meringue Gâteau

This recipe takes only five minutes to prepare but looks and tastes as though a lot of preparation went into it. The trick is to use really good vanilla ice cream. For a dinner party, slice the gâteau and place on individual plates, spoon ready-made strawberry or raspberry coulis around each slice and garnish with whole strawberries or raspberries.

SERVES SIX

400g/14oz/3½ cups mixed small strawberries, raspberries and/ or redcurrants

30ml/2 tbsp icing (confectioners') sugar

750ml/1¼ pints/ 3 cups vanilla ice cream

6 meringue nests or 115g/4oz meringue

1 Dampen a 900g/2lb loaf tin (pan) and line it with clear film (plastic wrap). If using strawberries, chop them into small pieces. Put them in a bowl and add the raspberries or redcurrants and icing sugar. Toss until the fruit is beginning to break up, but do not let it become mushy.

2 Put the ice cream in a bowl and break it up with a fork. Crumble the meringues into the bowl and add the soft fruit mixture.

3 Fold all the ingredients together until evenly combined and lightly marbled. Pack into the prepared tin and press down gently to level. Cover and freeze overnight. To serve, invert on to a plate and peel away the clear film. Serve in slices.

White Chocolate and Brownie Torte

This delicious dessert is easy to make and guaranteed to appeal to just about everyone. If you can't buy good quality brownies, use a moist chocolate sponge or make your own. For extra decoration, put a few fresh summer berries such as strawberries or raspberries around the edge or on the centre of the torte.

SERVES TEN

300g/11oz white chocolate, broken into pieces

600ml/1 pint/2½ cups double (heavy) cream

250g/9oz rich chocolate brownies

(unsweetened) cocoa powder, for dusting

1 Dampen the sides of a 20cm/8in springform tin (pan) and line with a strip of greaseproof (waxed) paper. Put the chocolate in a small pan. Add 150ml/¼ pint/⅔ cup of the cream and heat very gently until the chocolate has melted. Stir until smooth, then pour into a bowl and leave to cool.

2 Break the chocolate brownies into chunky pieces and sprinkle these over the base of the tin. Pack them down lightly to make a fairly dense base.

3 Whip the remaining cream until it forms peaks, then fold in the white chocolate mixture. Spoon into the tin to cover the layer of brownies, then tap the tin gently on the work surface to level the chocolate mixture. Cover and freeze overnight.

4 Transfer the torte to the refrigerator about 45 minutes before serving to soften slightly. Decorate with a light dusting of cocoa powder just before serving.

Juices and Drinks

FRESHLY MADE FRUIT AND VEGETABLE JUICES CAN ACT AS REFRESHING, REVITALIZING TONICS, WHILE FROTHY HOT CHOCOLATE OR VANILLA CAFFÉ LATTE CAN BE A RELAXING, INDULGENT TREAT. THIS CHAPTER IS PACKED WITH EASY-TO-MAKE DRINKS THAT CAN BE SIPPED AT LEISURE OR ENJOYED AS A PICK-ME-UP WHEN SPIRITS ARE FLAGGING.

Leafy Apple Lift-off

This delicious blend of fruit and fresh green leaves is refreshing and healthy. The leaves are robustly flavoured and have a peppery, pungent taste. To prepare the leaves, discard any damaged and discoloured ones and rinse thoroughly in cold water to remove any grit. To prevent the juice from being watery, dry the leaves in a salad spinner or on kitchen paper before juicing.

SERVES ONE

1 Quarter the apple. Using a juice extractor, juice the fruit and watercress, rocket or spinach.

2 Add the lime juice to the apple, grape and leaf mixture and stir thoroughly to blend all the ingredients together. Pour the juice into a tall glass and serve immediately.

1 eating apple

150g/5oz white grapes

25g/1oz watercress, rocket (arugula) or spinach

15ml/1 tbsp lime juice

Fennel Fusion

The hearty combination of raw vegetables and apples makes a surprisingly delicious juice that is packed with natural goodness and is a truly wonderful pick-me-up. Use the remaining cabbage and fennel to make a really crunchy salad – slice and dress with French dressing or simply with olive oil, herb vinegar and plenty of freshly ground black pepper and sea salt to taste.

SERVES ONE

1 Coarsely slice the red cabbage and the fennel bulb and quarter the eating apples. Using a juice extractor, juice the vegetables and fruit.

2 Add the lemon juice to the red cabbage, fennel and apple mixture and stir thoroughly to blend all the ingredients together. Pour into a glass and serve immediately.

½ small red cabbage

½ fennel bulb

2 eating apples

15ml/1 tbsp lemon juice

Tropical Calm

This deliciously scented juice is packed with goodness to cleanse and calm the system. Orange fruits such as cantaloupe melons and papayas are rich in the phytochemical betacarotene, which is a valuable antioxidant and is thought to have many health-promoting properties.

SERVES ONE

1 papaya

½ cantaloupe melon

90g/3½ oz seedless white grapes

1 Halve the papaya, remove the seeds and skin, then cut the flesh into coarse slices. Halve the melon, remove the seeds, cut into quarters, slice the flesh away from the skin and cut into chunks.

2 Using a juicer, juice the prepared fruit. Alternatively, blend the fruit in a food processor or blender for a thicker juice. Serve immediately.

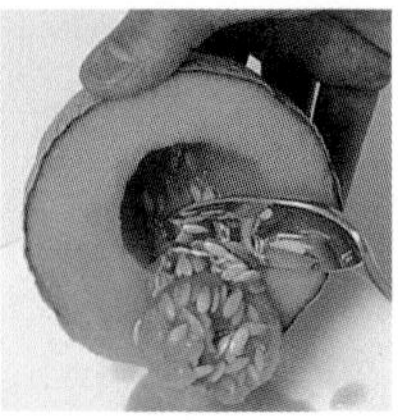

Strawberry Soother

Relax with this comforting blend of just two fruits – it is rich in vitamin C and fabulous flavour. It's a perfect drink for summer when sweet strawberries, peaches and necatarines are in season.

SERVES ONE

225g/8oz/2 cups strawberries

1 peach or nectarine

1 Hull the strawberries. Using a sharp knife, quarter the peach or nectarine and pull out the stone (pit). Cut the flesh into coarse slices or chunks.

2 Using a juice extractor, juice the fruit. Alternatively, place the fruit in a food processor or blender and process until smooth. Serve immediately.

Carrot Revitalizer

This vibrant combination of vegetables and fruit makes a lively, health-giving drink. Carrots yield generous quantities of sweet juice, which goes perfectly with the sharp flavour of pear and the zesty taste of orange. This powerful drink will nourish and stimulate the system.

SERVES ONE

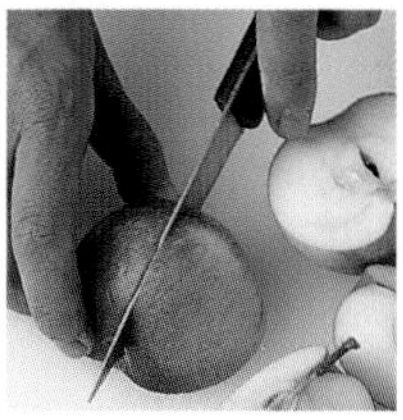

1 Scrub and trim the carrots and quarter the apples. Peel the orange and cut into rough segments.

2 Using a juice extractor, juice the carrots and fruit, pour into a glass and serve immediately.

3 carrots

2 apples

1 orange

Purple Pep

Jewel-coloured beetroot juice is well known for its detoxifying properties so this juice makes the perfect choice when you've been over-doing it. It offers an excellent supply of valuable nutrients that are essential for good health.

SERVES ONE

3 carrots

115g/4oz beetroot (beet)

25g/1oz baby spinach, washed and dried

2 celery sticks

1 Scrub and trim the carrots and beetroot. Using a sharp knife, cut the beetroot into large chunks.

2 Using a juice extractor, juice the carrots, beetroot, spinach and celery, then pour into a glass and serve immediately.

Melon Pick-me-up

Spicy fresh root ginger is delicious with melon and pear in this reviving and invigorating concoction. Charentais or Galia melon can be used instead of the cantaloupe melon in this recipe. To enjoy fresh root ginger at its best, buy it in small quantities and keep in a cool, dry place for up to a week. As it ages, the root will dry out and become hard.

SERVES ONE

½ cantaloupe melon

2 pears

2.5cm/1in piece of fresh root ginger

1 Quarter the cantaloupe melon, remove the seeds using a teaspoon or a sharp knife, and carefully slice the flesh away from the skin, reserving any juice. Quarter the pears and reserve any juice.

2 Using a juice extractor, juice the melon flesh and juice, quartered pears and juice and the fresh root ginger. Pour the juice into a tall glass and serve immediately.

Apple Shiner

This refreshing fusion of sweet apple, honeydew melon, red grapes and lemon provides a reviving burst of energy and a feel-good sensation. Serve as a drink or use to pour over muesli (granola) for a quick and healthy breakfast.

SERVES ONE

1 eating apple

½ honeydew melon

90g/3½oz red grapes

15ml/1 tbsp lemon juice

1 Quarter the apple and remove the core. Cut the melon into quarters, remove the seeds and slice the flesh away from the skin.

2 Using a juice extractor, juice the apple, melon and grapes. Alternatively, process the fruit in a food processor or blender for 2–3 minutes, until smooth. Pour the juice into a long, tall glass, stir in the lemon juice and serve immediately.

Citrus Sparkle

Zesty citrus fruits are packed with vitamin C, which is necessary for a healthy immune system. Pink grapefruit have a sweeter flavour than the yellow varieties – in fact, the pinker they are, the sweeter they are likely to be. For a lighter drink to serve two, divide the juice between two glasses and top up with sparkling mineral water or soda water (club soda) and ice cubes.

SERVES ONE

1 pink grapefruit

1 orange

30ml/2 tbsp freshly squeezed lemon juice

1 Cut the pink grapefruit and orange in half and squeeze out the juice using a citrus fruit squeezer.

2 Pour the juice into a glass, stir in 15ml/1 tbsp lemon juice, add the remaining lemon juice if required and serve immediately.

Hum-zinger

Aromatic tropical fruits make a drink that is bursting with flavour and energy. Enjoy a glass first thing in the morning to kick-start your day.

SERVES ONE

½ pineapple, peeled

1 small mango, peeled and stoned (pitted)

½ small papaya, seeded and peeled

1 Remove any "eyes" left in the pineapple, then cut all the fruit into fairly coarse chunks.

2 Using a juice extractor, juice the fruit. Alternatively, use a food processor or blender and process for about 2–3 minutes until smooth. Pour into a glass and serve immediately.

Strawberry and Banana Smoothie

The blend of perfectly ripe bananas and strawberries creates a drink that is both fruity and creamy, with a luscious texture. Papaya, mango or pineapple can be used instead of strawberries for a tropical drink. Popular with adults and children alike, this is a great way to get children to enjoy fruit – much healthier than commercial milkshakes, too.

SERVES FOUR

200g/7oz/1¾ cups strawberries, plus extra, sliced, to decorate

2 ripe bananas

300ml/½ pint/1¼ cups skimmed milk

10 ice cubes

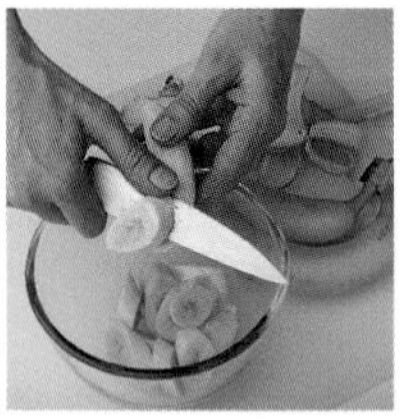

1 Hull the strawberries. Peel the bananas and chop them into fairly large chunks.

2 Put the fruit in a food processor or blender. Process to a thick, coarse purée, scraping down the sides of the goblet as necessary.

3 Add the skimmed milk and ice cubes, crushing the ice first unless you have a heavy-duty processor. Process until smooth and thick. Pour into tall glasses and top each with strawberry slices to decorate. Serve immediately.

EXTRAS

For a rich and velvety drink, add 120ml/4fl oz/½ cup coconut milk and process as above. Reduce the volume of milk to 175ml/6fl oz/¾ cup.

Raspberry and Orange Smoothie

Sharp-sweet raspberries and zesty oranges taste fabulous combined with the light creaminess of yogurt. This smoothie takes just minutes to prepare, making it perfect for breakfast – or any other time of the day. If you like a really tangy drink add freshly squeezed lemon or lime juice to taste.

SERVES TWO TO THREE

1 Place the raspberries and yogurt in a food processor or blender and process for about 1 minute, until smooth and creamy.

2 Add the orange juice to the raspberry and yogurt mixture and process for about 30 seconds, or until thoroughly combined. Pour into tall glasses and serve immediately.

COOK'S TIP

For a super-chilled version, use frozen raspberries or a combination of frozen summer berries such as strawberries, redcurrants and blueberries instead of fresh. You may need to blend the raspberries and yogurt slightly longer for a really smooth result.

250g/9oz/1½ cups fresh raspberries, chilled

200ml/7fl oz/scant 1 cup natural (plain) yogurt, chilled

300ml/½ pint/1¼ cups freshly squeezed orange juice, chilled

New York Egg Cream

No one knows precisely why this legendary drink is called egg cream, but some say it was a witty way of describing richness at a time when no one could afford to put both expensive eggs and cream together in a drink. Use full-fat (whole) milk for a really creamy taste. Dust a little cocoa powder over the top of the egg cream before serving, if you like.

SERVES ONE

45–60ml/3–4 tbsp good quality chocolate syrup

120ml/4fl oz/½ cup chilled milk

175ml/6fl oz/¾ cup chilled sparkling mineral water

1 Carefully pour the chocolate syrup into the bottom of a tall glass avoiding dripping any on the inside of the glass.

2 Pour the chilled milk into the glass on to the chocolate syrup.

3 Gradually pour the chilled sparkling mineral water into the glass, sip up any foam that rises to the top of the glass and carefully continue to add the remaining chilled sparkling mineral water. Stir well before drinking.

COOK'S TIP

An authentic egg cream is made with an old-fashioned seltzer dispenser that you press and spritz. In any case, you can use soda water (club soda) rather than mineral water, if you like.

Banana and Maple Flip

This satisfying drink is packed with so much goodness that it makes a complete breakfast in a glass – great for when you're in a hurry. Be sure to use a really fresh free-range egg. The glass can be decorated with a slice of orange or lime to serve.

SERVES ONE

1 small banana, peeled and halved

50ml/2fl oz/¼ cup thick Greek (US strained plain) yogurt

1 egg

30ml/2 tbsp maple syrup

1 Put the peeled and halved banana, thick Greek yogurt, egg and maple syrup in a food processor or blender. Add 30ml/2 tbsp chilled water.

2 Process the ingredients constantly for about 2 minutes, or until the mixture turns a really pale, creamy colour and has a nice frothy texture.

3 Pour the banana and maple flip into a tall, chilled glass and serve immediately. Decorate the glasses with an orange or lime slice, if you like.

COOK'S TIPS

- *To chill the drinking glass quickly, place it in the freezer while you are preparing the drink.*
- *For a hint of sharpness, add 5ml/1 tsp lemon or lime juice or use a slightly tangy yogurt.*

Vanilla Caffè Latte

This luxurious vanilla and chocolate version of the classic coffee drink can be served at any time of the day topped with whipped cream, with cinnamon sticks to stir and flavour the drink. Caffè latte is a popular breakfast drink in Italy and France, and is now widely available elsewhere.

SERVES TWO

700ml/24fl oz/scant 3 cups milk

250ml/8fl oz/1 cup espresso or very strong coffee

45ml/3 tbsp vanilla sugar, plus extra to taste

115g/4oz dark (bittersweet) chocolate, grated

1 Pour the milk into a small pan and bring to the boil, then remove from the heat. Mix the espresso or very strong coffee with 500ml/16fl oz/2 cups of the boiled milk in a large heatproof jug (pitcher). Sweeten with vanilla sugar to taste.

2 Return the remaining boiled milk in the pan to the heat and add the 45ml/3 tbsp vanilla sugar. Stir constantly until dissolved. Bring to the boil, then reduce the heat. Add the dark chocolate and continue to heat, stirring constantly until all the chocolate has melted and the mixture is smooth and glossy.

3 Pour the chocolate milk into the jug of coffee and whisk thoroughly. Serve in tall mugs or glasses topped with whipped cream and with cinnamon sticks to stir.

Frothy Hot Chocolate

Real hot chocolate doesn't come as a powder in a packet – it is made with the best chocolate you can afford, whisked in hot milk until really frothy. This recipe uses dark (bittersweet) chocolate, but for a special treat you could use Mexican chocolate, which is flavoured with almonds, cinnamon and vanilla, and sweetened with sugar. All the ingredients are crushed together in a special mortar, and heated over coals. The powdered mixture is then shaped into discs, which can be bought in specialist stores.

SERVES FOUR

1 litre/1¾ pints/ 4 cups milk

50–115g/2–4oz dark (bittersweet) chocolate, grated

1 vanilla pod (bean)

1 Pour the milk into a pan. Split the vanilla pod lengthways using a sharp knife to reveal the seeds, and add it to the milk; the vanilla seeds and the pod will flavour the milk.

2 Add the chocolate. The amount to use depends on personal taste – start with a smaller amount if you are unsure of the flavour and taste at the beginning of step 3, adding more if necessary.

3 Heat the chocolate milk gently, stirring until all the chocolate has melted and the mixture is smooth, then whisk with a wire whisk until the mixture boils. Remove the vanilla pod from the pan and divide the drink among four mugs or heatproof glasses. Serve the hot chocolate immediately.